GAMBLING AD

EXPLAINED

How to STOP Gambling
and Regain Control of your Life

JOHN WOODS

Although the author and publisher have made every effort to ensure that the information in this book was correct at press time, the author and publisher do not assume and hereby disclaim any liability to any party for any loss, damage, or disruption caused by errors or omissions, whether such errors or omissions result from negligence, accident, or any other cause.

This book is not intended as a substitute for the medical advice of physicians, therapist treatment or legal counsel.

First paperback edition 2022

A CIP catalogue record for this title is available from the British Library

ISBN 978-1-7397045-0-6 (paperback)
ISBN 978-1-7397045-1-3 (eBook)

www.GamblingAddictionExplained.com

CONTENTS

ACKNOWLEDGEMENTS

I would like to thank several people who have supported me at one time or another through my journey of addiction and recovery.

A special thank you to my incredible, wonderful, supportive, and very tolerant wife Nikk, for putting up with me for all these years. I would be truly lost without her and will love her until the end of time.

My children, Antony, and Melissa, who I am immensely proud of and who bring so much joy to my life. I love you both immensely.

My loving parents to whom I owe so much and are responsible for the best parts of my character.

To Christina Wright for proofreading my book and fine tuning some of the wording for me who deserves more credit for the production of this work than she will allow me to bestow.

To friends, old and new, past, and present, who have supported and encouraged me along the way. I am sure they will appreciate my honesty. Thank you to Jason Avery for reaching out to me in one of my darkest hours and giving me the kick up the backside I needed, R.I.P.

And finally to my weekly Gamblers Anonymous group who I have the utmost respect and gratitude for and who have been instrumental in my recovery.

1. HI. MY NAME IS JOHN, AND I AM A COMPULSIVE GAMBLER

After more than 30 years of gambling, I placed my final bet on January 5th, 2017.

I want to share the story of the anguish and pain my gambling addiction caused, how I finally overcame it, and the valuable lessons I've learnt since. My hope is that my honesty will give an understanding of gambling addiction to anyone affected by it, and most importantly, to help others experiencing harm through gambling to find their own way to stop.

I clearly recall as a toddler, someone lifting me up and standing me on a bar stool in front of a fruit machine. I remember watching the lights flashing and the symbols whirring by, as three lemons rolled in, then the winning coins clinking excitedly in the tray below. In Junior school, by the age of 8 or 9, I was regularly playing 'pitch and toss' at break time, for two pence pieces. Never played? It's simple; throw your coins against a wall - the player whose coin is nearest to the wall wins them all. Even then, I remember trying to convince school mates to raise the stakes and play with ten pence pieces. Ten pence was a lot of money to a 9-year-old in 1984. Age 11 and in senior school, we went on a residential trip and I was running a Blackjack game after lights out.

About this time, I really got into fruit machines; engrossed by the flashing lights, exciting features, and above all, the promise of a jackpot. There was a place in town, the 'Corner Pocket' which had pool tables, arcade games and 2 pence-a-play fruit machines with £2.00 jackpots. The thrill of skilfully hitting the right button at just the right time to get you onto that feature board and the promise it held was intoxicating. And there was the nudge-based bandit, with the chance to hit 10 nudges if you got the N, D and E on the win line. It was serious business; crouching down to peer intently through the glass so I could see through the reels and figure out how many nudges I needed for the best win. Or sometimes looking to see how full the hoppers which held the coins were and convincing myself they looked quite full, so it was surely going to pay out soon? Then, there was the buzz of hitting the gamble button for double or nothing - If you hit double, it paid to keep the button pressed in, then if you were quick and able enough, you'd take just enough pressure off before slamming it back down again. It was a skilful process, but the "Double" would stay lit and the winnings would go from 20 pence to 40 pence or 80 pence to £1.60.

What a rush it was. How exciting, how strangely at home I felt in that dingy place, spending hours of fun, mostly losing my money. Looking back now, I see that perhaps part of it was the buzz of having others crowding around to watch me play, making me feel both accepted and centre stage, especially as many of them were older. In all honesty, it was probably also the thrill and rush of doing something I knew my parents would not approve of or allow if they knew.

Ultimately though, the result was usually the same. I spent every penny I had on those fruit machines. Even back then I was incapable of walking out with any money remaining in my pockets. Even though the arcade was a good hour's walk from home, I would always end up walking because I never had enough money left for the bus. Even in the middle of winter, cold, dark, and raining, I would walk home. I was used to walking as every morning I was up early before school, and at weekends too, walking a couple of miles for my paper round. Sundays were always a killer with the Sunday magazines and supplements in the papers. There was so much extra on a Sunday, I had to carry two bags at once, one on each shoulder. All those early mornings, out in all weathers, walking miles to earn less than £5 a week. And for what? To blow it all in the 'Corner Pocket' on a Saturday.

When I was 15, I got a job in a local nightclub called Story's, collecting glasses on a Friday and Saturday night. I used to get paid at the end of the night on the Friday. On Saturday nights, on the way into work, I used to stop off in a dodgy restaurant not far from the nightclub. I wasn't interested in the food, but they had a fruit machine in there that I could play. At that time of night, the arcades were closed, and I was too young to go into a pub to play. Needless to say, I often spent all the wages I had picked up the night before, but at least the nightclub paid for a taxi home each night, so at least there was no long walk home.

At 17, I started an apprenticeship on the Railway, with British Rail as it was back then. I beat hundreds of applicants to get one of only three places available, and I was paid a massive £117.00 a week. Well, this was fantastic for my gambling. Not only did I now have real money to spend, but more importantly, I had access to more money – the joy of bank loans and credit cards. It was like all my Christmases had come at once. Now I could have a real go at this gambling lark, and with a decent amount of money to stake, I was surely going to start making it pay. I had plenty of cash now, what could possibly go wrong?

I was paid every four weeks on a Friday. By the time I had paid that month's loan repayments, credit card bills, payday loans and repaid money borrowed from friends, there was precious little left. What was left went on gambling, and that usually only lasted a couple of days. Soon, I was back to scheming up ways to get more money. Telling lies and sob stories to friends and family, more payday loans, an extension on the current bank loan or increase of credit on the visa, some dodgy deal on the side, whatever was necessary to get some more cash to get me over the next 3 or so weeks. And the cycle of misery continued on and on and on.

I would spend all my spare time in arcades, playing fruit machines, often three at once, positioning myself in the middle with one either side. I began spending more time in the bookies as my interest in betting on horses grew. I worked shifts, so I could often go before work, after work or even during work if I could get away with it. Even when I went to the pub with my friends, I would spend all night stood at the fruit machine and hardly any time actually socialising with them. If I sat down, it was only because I had spent up, or someone else was on the fruit machine. Even then I would still have half an eye on the machines, never fully engaged with my friends. If I heard a machine pay out, I would automatically count the sound of the coins hitting the tray and know exactly how much it had paid out. And I would always think, "Bastard!", because I had previously put all my money in so felt it was my money they were winning, or because I had not had chance to get onto the fruit machine to start with, so felt I had missed out.

Gambling was all I cared about. Gambling was all I thought and dreamt of. It consumed my every waking moment. As part of my apprenticeship, I attended Old Swan college in Liverpool, one day a week, to study Electrical Engineering. Unsurprisingly, I failed my second year because I spent my lunch time in the arcade around the corner and was often late back or missed lessons entirely. I would sometimes go to a pub in the area to play their fruit machines, but not too often as that meant wasting money on a drink.

By the age of 18, I realised I had a serious gambling problem, a problem I'd had for a long time. The debts, stress and pressures were mounting rapidly. I could see the way people looked at me, and I was ashamed of the person I was. I was ashamed of the way I behaved and the lies I told. I was lucky enough to be still living at home with my parents at the time. Any self-respect had gone. I don't remember the exact reason, perhaps it was because I'd had to admit that I had failed college and would have to repeat a year, but I eventually broke down and told my parents. When I say broke down, I literally mean fell to pieces, sobbing uncontrollably on the living room floor. I had hit my first, but unfortunately not my last, rock bottom in my life.

My parents were shocked, to put it mildly, and could not comprehend how I'd gotten to such a point. They were hard-working, church-going, frugal, careful people, who saved for everything. The only debt they'd ever had was their mortgage, which they worked hard to pay off as soon as possible. We never had a lot, but they always made sure my sister and I had what we needed, even if it was not always what we wanted. They had a small bet once a year on the Grand National and watched the race on the TV, but that was it as far as gambling went. And here I was, telling them I was in debt far beyond my means, which would take years to pay off because I'd gambled it all away. Until this point, they'd been proud to think I was working hard at my apprenticeship, doing well at college, and saving my money, just like they had always done. I can't imagine how it must have felt for them to realise that because of gambling I was on my last warning with work, failing at college, and had amassed a huge amount of debt with nothing to show for it.

They recognised it as a real problem, and wanting to help, arranged for me to see a psychiatrist who specialized in drug addiction. He prescribed medicines which were designed to inhibit the cravings that heroin addicts have for drugs. Don't forget, this was the early 1990s, and although gambling was a huge problem back then, it had not yet reached the epidemic proportions of today. Generally, people did not know what to do for a gambling addiction. The prescription drugs did not work for me and unfortunately my parents had wasted their money on the shrink. They had also researched Gamblers' Anonymous and found a meeting in Liverpool that I could attend.

Walking through the doors of a G.A. meeting for the first time is daunting to say the least. It takes a whole lot of courage to step over that threshold into the unknown. There were a multitude of worries running around my head - "What are the people going to be like? Will they judge me? Will they understand me? Will they be as awful as I am? Will I have to tell them what I have been doing? Do I have to stand up in front of a room full of people to tell them? What do I have to do at this meeting, what is expected of me? Will there be tea and biscuits?" A hundred and one other questions were racing around in there.

Well, the good thing is, it's a room full of people who do understand, and who do not judge. And there is usually tea and biscuits.

The first meeting I attended was in West Derby, Liverpool. I had a 30-minute train journey into Liverpool Lime Street, then a bus back out of the city centre to the suburbs. The meeting was held in a Church annex, and I remember walking around the outside of the Church trying to find it, feeling guiltily like I was skulking around and up to no good. I eventually found what I assumed was the right place, took a deep breath, pushed open the door and walked in.

The room was hazy with smoke and there were half a dozen men sat around a large oblong table. All of them were considerably older than me, more seasoned gamblers, you might say. Back then, I don't think they were used to seeing someone so young walk in. I was asked, by one of the men sat at the table in his broad, friendly, Scouse accent, "Can I help yer, Lad?"

I paused for a moment, not sure what to say. Could he help me? The small group of men sat patiently, looking at me, waiting for an answer.

"Is this G.A?" I stammered nervously.

"Yes lad. Come in. D'yer wanna brew?"

And just like that, I attended my first G.A meeting back in 1993. I was by far the youngest in the meetings then, and it was sometimes hard to relate to others within the group as they were all at least 20 years older than me. Remember, this was way before gambling had reached today's epidemic proportions, online gambling was not yet a thing. We were still 3 years away from the first real money online casino being launched by InterCasino. Unfortunately, since then online gambling has become extremely popular, and is so accessible, with every mobile phone capable of becoming a casino in your pocket. Today, I would not stand out for looking younger than other members; there are now a lot of people in their late teens and early twenties attending G.A.

I attended G.A. in Liverpool for about a year, managing to abstain from gambling for the majority of that time and getting my life back on track to some degree. However, I was not yet ready to be done with gambling, or gambling was not done with me.

So, after attending for a year, I proudly told my parents I no longer had a problem with gambling, and everything was going to OK. And to be fair, I believed that myself to some extent. I never told them I would never gamble again, just that I did not have a problem with it any longer. I think I naively did believe I could control it and have a little bet if I wanted to. I could take it or leave it. The arrogance of youth and the lack of respect for such an insidious addiction showed how immature I was. Within no time at all, I was gambling almost as much as I had ever done, but now with the added shame of knowing I had failed to give it up. I did not tell my parents. I foolishly thought I could not disappoint my parents a second time and put them through all that upset again.

Looking back, I really wish I'd had the strength to be honest with them, because not doing so only served to help convince me that I really had to keep it a secret from everyone, which made it so much harder to deal with. So, I never told them. Instead, I chose to continue down a deluded, damaging, and destructive path.

2. I KNOW I AM A DICKHEAD, BUT I LOVE AND RESPECT MYSELF

As I reached my early twenties, I was deep in tens of thousands of pounds of debt, and still had nothing to show for it but heartache and pain. At the time, I was fortunate enough to be in a fantastic job, still on the railway. I was involved with renewals work, which meant I had to work away from home at weekends when most major engineering work takes place. The problem was, I was off Monday to Friday most weeks, leaving me a huge amount of time on my hands, time to gamble. It was a well-paid job, £30000 a year basic, well above the average national wage in 1999. Despite that, I was still in huge amounts of debt as all my wages went on gambling or repaying the most urgent of my debts monthly, leaving me looking for more ways to get more cash to gamble more.

At the time, I'd moved into my girlfriend's house in Manchester. Although she knew I had a gambling problem; she never knew how bad it was because I kept the amount I was spending hidden. As it was her place, everything was in her name and I just helped towards the bills which were relatively low, so I was lucky in that respect. I never could have afforded my own place with the amount I was wasting gambling.

Monday to Friday, as soon as my girlfriend left for work, I would head into town to go to the arcades or bookies. There was one Arcade on Langworthy Road, Salford, which opened at 9am. By 8.59am, I used to be outside, waiting impatiently for it to open.

When the owner arrived, he would make us both a brew while I went around and turned on all the machines. He must have loved me, not only his best customer but doing his work for him too! To be fair though, he was a nice old boy and an old rocker, so we had a lot in common when it came to musical tastes and I enjoyed his company. Sometimes, just to switch it up a little, I'd go to the pub instead and nurse a solitary pint while playing the fruit machine all afternoon. My main vice was the fruit machines as it was a quicker fix than waiting for a horse race to start and finish. I would spend all day, pumping money in, pound coin after pound coin. I ended up with a repetitive strain injury in my right shoulder from the action of feeding pound coins in. Despite this, I would carry on and when the pain was too much, I'd awkwardly use my left hand instead. At the end of the day when I finally went home my hands would stink from handling the pound coin all day, it is a very unique and unpleasant smell. This was well before you could feed notes into the machines like you can today.

I would aim to be back home before my girlfriend returned from work, but usually only just made it back before her. If I was still out when she got home, I would lie about where I had been and what I had been doing rather than say I had been gambling all day. Often it would cause arguments, as the house would look the same as it had when she had left in the morning. Nothing done, no housework, no odd jobs done, dishes still in the sink, washing still needed doing, a stack of ironing getting bigger by the day. She couldn't understand how I was at home all day with nothing to do, and not be able to help with the things that needed doing around the house. She was out working all day and would have to come home to everything I hadn't done. Or she would have to get the household chores done at the weekend, while I was away working, instead of just having a relaxing weekend off.

Fortunately for our relationship, it was not like that all the time, as I was paid four weekly, I usually only had money to gamble with for the first week or so out of the four. If I was totally out of money and could not get any more, I would do more of the things around the house but probably still not enough. And even then, I would want to be praised for it and expect her to be thankful when it was the least that I could have been doing.

The truth was my gambling at this point was too much for me to manage. It was totally taking over my life. Worst still, it was causing arguments with the woman I loved, and I was hardly seeing any of my friends or family. Any spare money or time was wasted gambling and I was working away most weekends, meaning a weekend off was rare, so it was hard from that point of view too. It got to the point that I resented my job because I was having to be away at the weekend while my friends would be doing normal weekend fun activities and I was missing out. It also meant I could not take my girlfriend out at the weekend either. Not that I would have often had the money to do anything anyway. And the worst part was despite all the weekends given up working I had nothing to show for it because all my money was wasted gambling. Worryingly, I was constantly lying about finances and what I was doing with my spare time and money. I was more and more depressed about the hold gambling had on me, and I could not see how I could stop.

I was ashamed of myself and the grip the gambling addiction had. The number of times I would come out of an arcade or bookies having spent all my money, often money I should have been using for something else and swear to myself that it was the last time. No more. I had to stop gambling because it was ruining my life. Then the next day I would get up and do it all again. At this point, I was wretched, full of self-loathing and believing that the world and everyone in it would be better off without me. Fortunately, despite my suicidal thoughts, I never got as far as putting together a suicide plan. It's so hard to explain what it is like desperately wanting to stop doing something but being totally under the control of an addiction and unable to. I knew I had to do something soon before it was too late.

It was at this point that I turned to Hypnotism to try to find a remedy for this horrific addiction that was ruining my life. I know some people are sceptical of hypnotism, and I am certain some hypnotists are better than others. I have to say the one I saw was incredible and helped me immensely at the time. His name was Peter and I do not know if he still practices as this was back in the beginning of 2000. I had many sessions over a few months and I really enjoyed them, I always came out feeling positive and confident. Most importantly, I stopped gambling after my very first session.

Peter was not a one trick pony using just hypnotism to help me though, he combined it with EFT (Emotional Freedom Technique) and NLP (Neuro-linguistic programming). Neuro-linguistic programming is a way of changing someone's thought patterns and behaviours to help achieve their desired outcomes. NLP therapists achieve this by working with people to help them understand their thinking, behavioural patterns, emotions, and aspirations. The therapist can help them find and strengthen the skills that they have which serve them best and help them in developing new strategies to replace the unproductive, damaging ones.

The Emotional Freedom Technique is also known as Tapping. Based on Chinese medicine, there are thought to be several points of the body where energy flows through, called meridian points. It is believed a disruption in one's energy causes negative emotions and pain. By tapping these meridian points, the flow of energy is restored, in much the same way that acupuncture works. While tapping each point you repeat the following phrase, or something similar, out loud before moving onto the next meridian point. "I know I am a (insert word that best describes you) but I love and accept myself".

Now the only thing is, the first time I did this exercise, I could not think of a single word that best described myself and my problem. Peter had a way around this though. "I want you to think about who you are and what you do and then I am going to tap you on the forehead and a word will spring to mind that best describes you. Say that word out loud immediately, and that is the word we shall use today".

So that is what Peter did, and the word that at once sprang out of my mouth was Dickhead. In fairness, that was an accurate, honest description of me at that time. So, I spent the next 5 or 10 minutes tapping my meridian points and saying repeatedly, "I know I am a Dickhead, but I love and accept myself" while Peter struggled to keep a straight face. Luckily, as time went by and I was starting to feel better about myself, I found a different word to use for that exercise.

I saw Peter several times over a period of 6 months, weekly for the first 2 months, then twice a month before finishing on a couple of monthly visits. Each visit would last usually 30 to 45 minutes but sometimes, in the earlier stages, I would be there for maybe an hour. Thanks to those 6 months of therapy, I stopped gambling completely for the best part of 18 months and started to get my life back in order and made a dent in some of the debts I had.

Once again, I believed I had control of my gambling addiction. Once again, I was wrong.

3. FINALLY WAKING UP TO MY DELUSIONS OF BEING IN CONTROL

n April 2001 I married my amazing wife who is, incredibly, despite all I have put her through, still with me today. It was one of the happiest days of my life with only two others to rival it since, those being the days that my two wonderful children were born.

I naively believed I had beaten my gambling addition, so decided to go to Doncaster Races for my Stag 'Do. I figured I could go to the races and have a cheeky bet on the horses just like normal people did. If I stayed away from the fruit machines, which I genuinely had no interest in since my Hypnotherapy, I'd be fine. So I went to Doncaster, had a great time and did not go crazy. It was all good. I felt in control now of the gambling and not the other way around. After that success I went to Aintree Racecourse for Ladies' Day, the day before my wedding. Again, I felt in control, so much so that I left before the last race started to make sure I caught the train home at a sensible time, so I would be well rested for my big day. Gambling was no longer a problem for me, I was its master and I could take it or leave it, just like normal people could. At least that is what I convinced myself to believe. In truth, that is not how it was at all. The truth was, I was beginning a long, slow journey back to despair which I could not, or would not, see. I now realise that I was transitioning into what you could call a functioning compulsive gambler.

Changing tack, I was still trying to convince myself I could make gambling pay and now thought horse-racing was the way to do it.

After all, I had been to two race meetings and not gone crazy. Surely that was a good sign? To that end, in 2002 I started my own website offering horse racing tips - JohnsProBets.com. Soon, I had hundreds of people logging in daily to see if there was a bet worth placing or not. I would spend 5 or 6 hours a day studying form to find a suitable bet and if I could not find one then I would not bet. If I found a horse worth betting on, I would put £100 on to win, or £50 each way. Over a year, I made 60 level stake points (LSP) profit, in other words £6000. Now that looks OK at first glance, but if I asked you to work 5 or 6 hours a day, for 6 or 7 days a week, for £6000 a year, you would quite rightly tell me to sod off. Regardless, I never saw that £6000 at the end of the year because I had frittered it away throughout the year. By now, I was treating myself to the odd visit to an arcade with the intention of only spending £20 or £30. Not going every day or every other day like I used to, maybe just once a week or so. But of course, I never spent just £20 or £30, it was always more like £200 or £300. And I would come out kicking myself and swearing that I would not do it again, that it was just a slip up, but of course I did do it again, many, many times. The only place that £6000 existed was on a spread sheet I kept track of my bets on, it was certainly not in my bank account. I ran the website for just under two years before giving it up. I was not only becoming disenchanted with the amount of work it took, but also my actual job changed so I no longer had the required time to spend on it.

Next move? I convinced myself that I could make Online Poker pay. I could play Poker to a reasonable level and often played a very disciplined game on low-stake tables. £1/£2 up to £3/£6 blinds but sometimes higher stake tables - £10/£20 depending how confident I was feeling and how big my pot was at the time. I could make around £1000 over the course of a week or so playing tight Poker, but would inevitably end up losing the lot, often in a very short space of time. You see, at this point the gambling addiction was well and truly creeping back into my life, although at the time, I was in severe denial and I have only realised that since stopping gambling.

I could play my A game all week and amass a nice little pot then blow the lot by getting a bad beat and going on tilt. My discipline would begin to crumble and I would play too many hands that I had no right to get involved in. I either wanted the action of being in the game, or I started chasing the losses, playing poor starting hands that I should have folded. Kenny was right, "You've got to know when to hold 'em. Know when to fold 'em".

The online poker companies obviously were not happy just taking a rake from the pot, greedy little monsters that they are, so they introduce enticing links for Blackjack or Roulette. These open a smaller window in the corner of the screen, allowing me to gamble away my money more quickly whilst playing poker at the same time. In my skewed, gambling mind, that was OK because at least I was not losing too much via Poker, so I could maintain the self-delusion that I could make it pay playing Poker. So some weeks I would be thousands up, and other weeks back down again. Because I thought I would win money if I just maintained my A game, or avoided the bad beats, it seemed sensible to get a small loan or increase the credit on the Visa because I was going to win it back and then some. The problem was, I did this several times and of course each time larger than the last. Even in defeat, I convinced myself I was good at

Poker because I had worked out what hand my opponent had before they showed it. Sometimes I knew I was beat but felt I had to pay to see them just to be sure instead of folding.

When my son was a baby and did not sleep through the night, I used to sit up with him cradled in my arm while playing Poker online. My wife might have thought I was a superstar, being up with him so she could get some sleep. I did enjoy that time together, don't get me wrong, but my overriding thought as he stirred and I jumped out of bed was that I could now play an hour or so of Poker online. My son would often be fast asleep in my arms but I would play on instead of putting him down in his cot and going back to bed myself. I am sure this is a familiar story to many gamblers all over the world. I wonder how many people I was playing at the time were sat with their own babies in their arms too?

So despite my delusions of control, of being able to make gambling pay in some way, my debts continued to grow. I was now not only lying to other people, but I was also lying to myself. Over the following years I would pay off a loan or a credit card or at least reduce the balance a bit only to top it up, increase it further or get a bigger loan. I would justify this by telling myself I needed to so I could pay for a family holiday or the car insurance that needed renewing, or I had just gotten a bit behind with things and needed a cash boost to get straight. I would blame the fact on not earning enough money in my current job and until I found a better one or got promoted what else was I supposed to do? Yes, I accepted that I sometimes had the odd slip, ending up in an arcade or bookies. Yes, I had a blowout sometimes spending too much money, but it was not as often as it used to be. Yes, I sometimes sat up playing at online casinos half the night while my wife and children were asleep upstairs, but it wasn't that often. Well the truth was I would block out exactly how often that was because I did not want to know. I stopped looking at my bank statements because I did not want to know how bad it really was. I knew I was always overdrawn and seldom got out of the overdraft as my monthly wage was never as much as my overdraft limit which I had maxed out at £4500.

And so, like every other compulsive gambler, I was also, once again, a compulsive liar. Telling lies to myself, to my family, to my friends. Telling lies about my finances and about where I was going and what I was doing. The truth is, I have lied to everyone I have ever loved, including my children.

So essentially, if you've stayed this far, you'll recognise a story like any other compulsive gambler, mounting debts, lies, self-loathing, numerous rock bottoms promising myself never again. A vicious cycle of sating the gambling addiction and having a bet, then eventually losing, and feeling anger, frustration, shame, and despair. To escape the feeling of despair we lose ourselves in the escapism of the gambling dream world only to begin the cycle once more. And so it goes on, and on, and on.

I finally broke my cycle of despair in early January 2017. Sitting in my car, in a hotel car park, early hours of the morning. Why wasn't I tucked up in bed? Well, I couldn't get a phone signal in the hotel room while away on a training course. I had just lost £900 that I could not afford to lose, in the blink of an eye, on an online slot game on my phone. I had done it again, and I was sick to death of it and full of self-loathing. I could not take any more, gambling had me beat, in fact it had beaten me black and blue for most of my life and I could not carry on. I had hit rock bottom hundreds of times over the many years of gambling and swore I would never gamble again, only to get up the next day and start all over again. This time was different, I was completely exhausted with it all and I just could not carry on any longer. I posted the following to a private group on social media for people with depression or anxiety that I was part of:

"Sometimes I loathe myself. Like today. I am such a dick. I am so self-destructive which would almost be ok but my self-destructive streak will also eventually hurt the ones I love. I can't tell the one I love most of all for this very reason. I don't expect advice or anyone to tell me I am a great guy. I know for the most part I am. But I wish I could exercise old demons and addictions once and for all."

I got about 30 comments after that, mostly from people I did not know, offering kind words of support, and some from friends who reassured me that I was indeed a great guy and sending me love. One good friend, Jason Avery, called me the next day and asked me what was going on. I told him I had been gambling again and it was out of control and I did not know what to do, and I couldn't take much more. He told me I had to tell my wife everything and ask for her help because I obviously could not beat this alone. I told him no way; she would be furious. Even the thought of telling her filled me with dread. She thought I had beaten my problem with gambling years ago, if I told her the truth now she would know I had been lying to her for years. Jason told me I had no choice and I had to do it and accept whatever I had coming. So I drove home all the way from Bletchley where I had been staying, about a 5 hour drive in awful traffic, with a gut wrenching sensation, stomach churning, dreading the conversation to come, but convinced Jason was right. Jason reaching out to me, at one of the darkest moments of my life, and giving me the strength to do what I had to do, along with his subsequent support, was a pivotal moment in my life. I did not realise it at the time though. It was only after reminiscing when I heard the sad news of his passing that I did. I never got the chance to thank him for his gift that day. Rest easy my friend.

When I walked through the door both my kids were excited to see me and had lots to tell me about what they had been up to while I was away. Especially my daughter, who was at that point still in the habit of running up to give me a big cuddle as soon as I walked in, (I miss those days). So despite the heaviness in my heart about the conversation to come, I acted as though everything was OK until I put the kids to bed some hours later. We compulsive gamblers, after all, are accomplished liars and actors.

I then came downstairs and closed the living room door which is something we never used to do when the kids where in bed so my wife knew immediately something was wrong. I told her I had something to tell her, that I had been gambling again, in fact that I had never really stopped and it was out of control. I told her everything, all of it, about the debts I still had, about all the online gambling accounts and about all the numerous times I had lied and said I was working late or doing something when I was actually in the bookies or arcade. She didn't start shouting or get angry like I had been dreading. I wish she had, but her reaction to my revelation was worse still. I will never forget the look of hurt on her face, the disappointment and worry in her eyes, her whole body seem to sag as the realisation set in of what I was saying to her. She had thought this insidious gambling addiction of mine had been dealt with years ago and now she understood not only had it not but that I had been lying to her for years. It is a hard thing to see such pain and disappointment in the face of the woman you love and harder still knowing you are the reason for it. I told her how sorry I was and I promised I was going to get control and that I would start going to G.A. meetings again.

The next day at work, my wife sent a link to the address and times of the local G.A. group in my town which as it happened was that very night. I am extremely fortunate to have such a wonderful, supportive, and understanding wife. She has stood by me and helped me and I know not everyone has that in their lives and I am extremely grateful.

So that night I walked into my first G.A. meeting in over 20 years. I decided on the way there that I would probably not say much, if anything at all, and I would probably only attend the once. Surely one meeting would be enough to give me a kick up the arse and remind me of all the reasons I needed to control my gambling. Of course this was the addiction already whispering in my ear, telling me my gambling was not that big a problem and a G.A. meeting would be the quick fix I needed to get back on track. But the truth is, there is only one way to control gambling for a problem or compulsive gambler and that is to stop all together.

With some difficulty, I found the place I was after which was not easy and I almost gave up and went the pub instead. It was in a separate building tucked away at the back of the address I had taken from the G.A. website. Ten minutes after the meeting had started, I walked into the building. I could see some people in a room to the right, sat around a table. I figured this must be it and opening the door, sheepishly asked if this was Gamblers Anonymous. Thankfully it was, and a wonderful chap called Steve who was chairing welcomed me in with a smile and a handshake and immediately put me at ease. There were only four other men sat around the table, one of who has become a friend of mine called Andy who still goes the same meeting as me. In fact I have made some fantastic friends through G.A. It was a very different feel from the last time I had attended G.A nearly 20 years before, for a start there was not a thick haze of cigarette smoke over the table. There were smiles all round and welcoming nods as I pulled up a chair and sat down.

I remember listening to the stories or 'therapies' as they are called, from each person in turn around the table and was surprised at how many of their stories rang true with me and my experiences. There were so many details or elements of each story, while different from mine, that I could easily relate to. Eventually it came around to my turn and Steve asked me if I wished to say anything, that I did not have to, but it was generally best if people tried to share at least a little on their first visit. So I decided I would speak after all and boy, once I started, it seemed like I could not stop. The whole story came out all the way from my early childhood days of gambling to the present day. It all just came flooding out, all the pain, the grief, the shame, the stupidity, the lies, and the despair that gambling had caused me and those around me. Considering I had been doubtful that I would even speak, I was amazed at how much I did when it had come to it, it felt as though I was going on for ever. All the time the others in the room sat patiently waiting and listening to my story.

When I finally finished speaking I felt like a massive weight had been lifted from me, I did not realise just how much this awful addiction had been crushing me until that moment. Steve and the other guys thanked me for sharing my story with them and that they could relate to what I had told them and they understood. They assured me I was in the right place and that I could stop gambling by taking it one day at a time and attending the meetings. I felt the weight lift further as I realised that I believed them, that I knew at that moment there was hope after all and that I could and would stop gambling.

I left that meeting feeling elated and knew I was definitely going to be back the next week and I have been virtually every week since early January 2017. And I have not had a bet since, one day at a time.

4. COMPULSIVE AND PROBLEM GAMBLING

Many view gambling as a form of harmless entertainment, a bit of fun to be had with friends. They stay away from high stake bets or spending more than they can afford and limit both the time and money they spend on gambling. Many people do not gamble at all, they simply have no interest in it or think it is a waste of money. But for some, gambling becomes an addiction and destroys their life, and the lives of those close to them.

In this book I talk about 'compulsive or pathological gambling' and 'problem gambling' and it is important to try to explain the difference between the two. Compulsive or pathological gambling is at the extreme end of things and very definitely an addition. Problem gamblers or At Risk Gamblers, while still a major concern, may not necessarily have problems in every aspect of their lives caused by gambling, only some, but they are at risk of developing into full blown addicts. In both cases there is an urge to gamble continuously despite their desire to stop and the negative consequences it causes in a person's life.

Compulsive or Pathological gambling is a chronic, progressive disorder which will only get worse if unchecked, but can be controlled if action is taken and support sought. A compulsive Gambler will not be able to stop without support and help. A problem Gambler will often be able to stop if the motivation is great enough such as the danger of their loved one leaving them, the realisation that mounting debts are unmanageable or the threat of losing their job. A compulsive or Pathological Gambler will be unable to stop without help despite these reasons as they are under the control of the addiction. Compulsive or problem gambling can both lead to financial ruin, the loss of employment, loss of homes, loss of self-respect, the end of relationships with loved ones, ill health both physical and mental, self-harming, depression, and suicide. There is also frequently a link with drug or alcohol misuse as a means of coping with the stress, anxiety and depression caused by gambling which often in itself triggers the desire to gamble ensuring the cycle continues.

Many institutions simply refer to both Compulsive or Problem Gamblers by using the generic term of Problem Gambler or Problem Gambling. So if I switch from one to the other when referencing different reports from around the world or in the telling of one of my personal tales, do not be too concerned. I am just trying to give a general overview of Gambling Addition in this book and explain it as best I can, based upon my own addiction and my experiences on my road to recovery. It is important to remember I am not an academic, doctor, psychologist, or counsellor. I am just John, a Compulsive Gambler who has been successful at stopping to Gamble and I want to share what I have learned along the way.

Gamblers Anonymous have a questionnaire with 20 questions used as a self-diagnosis tool to determine if someone is a compulsive gambler. If you answer yes to 7 or more questions it is considered you are in fact a compulsive gambler. Unfortunately I was able to answer yes to 20 out of 20.

The South Oaks Gambling Screen (SOGS) is a screen popular in America used to measure pathological gambling. This asks 16 questions related to many gambling behaviours and how the person feels about their gambling behaviours. SOGS then classifies individuals into one of three categories: non-problem gambler, problem gambler and probable pathological gambler. Other popular screens are the Diagnostic and Statistical Manual of Mental Disorders (DSM-IV) and the Problem Gambling Severity Index (PGSI).

All these screens or questionnaires can be found online for you to check out. However, in my opinion, if one or more of the following statements apply to you or a loved one then there exists a serious gambling problem which needs addressing immediately.

1. There are concerns about the time spent gambling and it is considered excessive.

2. There is an inability to control the amount of money spent while gambling.

3. When not gambling there is an overpowering urge to gamble which preoccupies thoughts.

4. Gambling causes harm in any area of life but especially finances, health or relationships with friends and family.

Reports using both DSM-IV and PGSI screens produced on behalf of the Gambling Commission in the U.K suggest that compulsive gambling in the UK population aged 16+ is anywhere between 350000 and 430000 people nationally. Not to mention the estimated 55000 children already addicted to gambling which is extremely frightening. In addition to this it is estimated in the U.K that there are a further 2 million at risk gamblers for which gambling is causing problems in their lives. It is no wonder it is such a profitable business for the gambling industry with £14.2 bn total gross gambling yield (GGY) in Great Britain (Apr 2019 – Mar 2020).

Gambling is not just a problem in the U.K however, it is very much a global thing.

In America the National Council on Problem Gambling (NCPG) estimates that approximately 2 million, 1% of U.S adults, to be pathological or compulsive gamblers. A further 4 to 6 million U.S adults, 2% - 4%, are considered to be problem gamblers. Of U.S. residents aged 14-21, approximately 2.1% struggle with problem gambling while another 6.5% are at-risk. In 2018 it was estimated that the U.S commercial casino gaming revenue was approximately $41.7 billion while the Indian casinos brought in about $33.7 billion. The frightening thing is that this is with the vast majority of states having restrictions on gambling to some degree essentially making it "illegal" according to their State Law. Almost all states have laws that ban at least some form of gambling, particularly sports betting and online. It is a complicated topic but more and more states are looking at making more forms of gambling legal and logically it follows that more people will develop serious gambling problems as that access is increased. My concern would be that each state will not be ready for this and have suitable services and support for the gambling harm yet to come.

Gambling in Australia is a huge problem, especially with poker machines known as Pokies which are allowed in any pub or club, except for Western Australia where they are kept to casinos. Despite Australia having only 0.3% of the world's population it is estimated it has nearly 200,000 or 18% of the world's poker machines. Australians lose around $23 billion each year on gambling, around $14 billion of this on Pokies.

Around 80,000 to 160,000 (or 0.5 - 1.0%) of Australian adults experience significant problems gambling and a further 250,000 to 350,000 (or 1.4 - 2.1% of adults) experience moderate risks that may make them vulnerable to problem gambling. However the Australian Institute of Family Studies found that 1.39 million Australian adults had experienced one or more gambling-related problems(data from 2015). Australians have the highest loss per adult $ figures in the world at over $1200, with Singapore, Ireland, and Canada close behind. But these are not the only places where gambling is a huge problem, it is affecting hundreds of millions of people worldwide.

In all instances when it comes to these figures I cannot help but think, if anything, there are far more problem gamblers than these reports suggest. The reason being that it is such a secretive addiction and so easily hidden from most people that I still believe there are many more people suffering gambling harm than yet known.

5. WHY DO SOME PEOPLE BECOME PROBLEM GAMBLERS?

W hy do some people become addicted to gambling or develop a gambling problem? That is an important question but not one easily answered. It is believed generally in Gamblers Anonymous that it is not particularly important to know why a compulsive gambler gambles. And to a point I agree, the most important thing is to stop and you do not initially need to know why you did it in the first place to stop. However this book has been written to try and shed some light on gambling addiction for both the gambler and their family and friends who are also affected. I really want to try and explain gambling addiction and some of the potential reasons behind it. If the gambler can understand what has not only led them to this addiction but what it is that keeps hold of them they can begin to develop some strategies to help them combat it. Most importantly the gambler can then understand that it is not their fault they have a gambling addiction, they are not a bad person. Understanding that it is not their fault takes a huge weight off their shoulders and begins to remove that guilt that they carry. However not being their fault does not mean it is not their responsibility to deal with the Gambling Problem or Addiction. It very definitely is.

There are numerous reasons or contributing factors as to why someone might become addicted to gambling or at least develop enough of a problem with gambling that it causes them or others harm in some way. I will share some of the more common ones and give my own thoughts on them. There will be others but I will just review the more widely accepted potential causes. Gambling addiction is a very complicated business and in many cases there will be multiple reasons behind a person's gambling problem and not just one.

Illness.

Many people refer to addictions as an illness and I certainly consider gambling addiction to be an illness. The very definition of illness in the dictionary is a disease or period of sickness affecting the body or mind. Compulsive gambling, or gambling disorder, is the uncontrollable urge to carry on gambling despite the harm it does to both the gambler and other people in their life. In this way it very definitely has a negative effect on both the gambler's body and mind.

Gambling addiction is often known as the Hidden Illness or Addiction as its symptoms are not usually visible like those of an Alcohol or Drug addiction.

In 2013, the Diagnostic and Statistical Manual of Mental Disorders (DSM-5) included gambling as a diagnosable disorder. This shows there is enough evidence from studies and research carried out to show Compulsive Gambling is an illness or mental health condition and not just a lack of willpower.

The World Health Organisation (WHO) has long classed gambling as a disorder due to its addictive behaviours associated with functional impairment or distress. It is now widely accepted that gambling addiction falls under mental health illness. WHO estimate there are

350 million problem gamblers in the world. Many compulsive gamblers, due to the secretive nature of their illness, think that there is no one else like them with such a terrible problem and that they are alone. This estimate shows just how wrong that kind of thinking is. You are very definitely not alone. Perhaps more frightening still though is that it is estimated, on average, that compulsive or pathological gamblers negatively affect between 6 and 10 people in their lives. Usually family and friends but also complete strangers they come across in the form of crime committed to fund gambling habits for example. Moderate or at risk gamblers will negatively affect less people than this in their lives but will affect some. So in fact it is likely that problem gambling negatively affects or causes harm to well over 1 billion people worldwide. That is a staggering amount of people.

- *So is gambling an illness? Yes, absolutely it is, in fact I would go as far as to say we are in a gambling pandemic.*

- *Fortunately, it is an illness which can be managed successfully just like many other illnesses given the right support and help.*

Dopamine hits.

One of the contributing factors to a person becoming addicted to gambling is the reward system in our brain being short-circuited, and diminished functioning of the cognitive control circuitry in the brain. Studies in Neuroscience, Genetics and Psychology have shown that a series of circuits or neural pathways in our brain link various regions together such as memory, pleasure, motivation, and movement. This is known as the Reward System and its main job is to keep us alive and make sure we pass on our genes. It does this by encouraging us to create habits which are critical to meeting these goals, so things like having sex and eating a good meal. When we engage in an activity that is beneficial to our survival and that of the human race, our reward system releases a chemical, called Dopamine, making us feel good and so encourages us to make more of a habit of these activities. It has been discovered that it can be triggered by gambling and in Pathological Gamblers more is released than healthy control subjects without an addiction to gambling. In fact, it has been shown that addictions can trigger the reward system to releasing up to ten times the normal amount of Dopamine.

You might wonder. "But gambling does not keep me alive so why the hell is the reward system engaged when I do?" - Great question.

The reward system is one of the most primitive parts of our brains and goes back to when we were hunter-gatherers. We had to go out there and find or hunt our food with an uncertainty about if our efforts would be rewarded and to what extent, if any. Our brains are designed to take risks and seek rewards for survival even if the outcome is uncertain, in fact it does this even if the outcome is repeatedly negative. In the same way the reward system releases Dopamine so does another system called the Uncertainty Reward system creating a strong source of motivation to carry out tasks when the outcome is unknown. If it was not for this we would not have bothered getting up in the morning and leaving the cave. This would explain why we chase loses and continue to gamble. Of course these functions are no longer needed for survival but it is possible gambling has hijacked the reward system for some people.

The problem is, the more the brain is exposed to Dopamine, especially high levels, the less responsive it becomes to its effect. In other words it builds up a tolerance needing more and more to be effective. So like a person with an addictive drug problem needing to take bigger hits and more often, gamblers need to take bigger risks and more often. The double whammy is that while this is going on and our brains are awash with Dopamine the balance is shifted from our Prefrontal Cortex to our reward system. The Prefrontal Cortex is responsible for the cognitive control circuitry in the brain helping us to tame impulses, predict consequences of our actions, plan or set goals and manage our emotional reactions. Stress can also have a negative effect on the Prefrontal Cortex and I would suggest everyone with a gambling problem or addiction suffers from stress whether they realise it or not. So the more you get stressed, the more your brain shifts the focus from the functions of your Prefrontal Cortex to the more primitive areas of your brain. Again this is a natural occurrence, dating back to our primitive age. Back then being under stress probably meant you were either hunting your dinner or running away from something hunting you for its dinner. So depending which scenario it was your brain was either priming the reward system or engaging the fight or flight system.

In severe gambling addiction, people can also go through withdrawal just like with drug addiction. If their brain is deprived of a dopamine-stimulating substance or activity for too long they begin to feel physically ill, can get the shakes and struggle to sleep. This again causes considerable stress which in turn has a negative effect on your Prefrontal Cortex. In the height of my gambling addiction I certainly struggled to sleep, in fact I would say I was an insomniac.

At the time I blamed the fact that I worked shifts but looking back I was probably going through withdrawals on a regular basis when the money ran out.

All of this makes it very difficult to stop, but not impossible once you begin to understand what is going on with your brain. Your brain has made a mistake in assigning both importance and a necessity to gambling. The good news is your addictive brain still has plasticity and can develop new neural pathways; this is known as Neuroplasticity. When you know what is going on you can force yourself to think logically about what is happening to you. Once your dopamine washed brain has had chance to recover your overactive reward system will drop back to the levels it once was and you can concentrate on having it engage with new healthier activities. As you engage with these healthier activities you develop new neural pathways immediately which become stronger the more you use them. In turn the old destructive neural pathways of addiction will begin to weaken. It is truly an incredible thing; you can actually change the way your brain works.

- *You do not have to accept that your brain is wired a certain way and that there is nothing you can do about it.*

- *It is within your power to change it for the better and achieve fantastic things including a gamble free life.*

Pharmaceutical side effects.

There is a proven link between specific prescription medicines and antidepressants that affect dopamine activity in the brain and cause addiction to gambling. The type of drugs that do this are known as dopamine antagonists and can be used to treat, amongst other conditions, Restless Leg Syndrome, Parkinson's Disease, Bipolar Disorder, Depression and Anxiety. Whilst these side effects are known to exist and awareness is improving, it is unlikely that many doctors prescribing the medications enquire if their patient has suddenly developed a serious gambling problem since beginning treatment. They will no doubt be more concerned about checking on how it is affecting their specific complaint. The patient is also not likely to want to discuss their newfound gambling problem with their doctor and without being properly informed about potential side effects are unlikely to link the two in the first place. There once was a man who came to my local G.A group who did have Restless Leg Syndrome and was prescribed a dopamine antagonist medication for it, despite his doctor knowing he was a recovering gambler. The poor gambler reverted to his old ways, only later discovering the side effect of his medication.

The last time I saw him at a meeting he was considering pursuing legal action against his doctor. That was some time ago and I do not know if he followed it up as he stopped coming to the meeting but I sincerely hope that making the doctor aware of the situation will prevent further cases in future for his patients.

- *If you feel your medication is causing you to gamble or are already a gambler going onto new medication which has side effects that may make matters worse, then a conversation needs to happen with your doctor.*

- *Never just stop taking medication though without consulting your doctor as this could be dangerous to your health.*

Hereditary.

There have been several studies of families in relation to gambling disorders, parents, and siblings and whether it is something that runs in the family. A University of Iowa study confirms that pathological gambling does run in families. They assessed 95 pathological gamblers and 91 control subjects as well as 1075 family members, parents, brothers, and sisters. They found that 11% of the gambler's relatives were also pathological gamblers themselves compared to 1% of the relatives of control subjects without a gambling disorder. This means that the odds are about eight times higher in gambling families for pathological gambling to run in those families when compared to control families.

There have been at least three major studies into twins and gambling disorders, the largest of which was carried out in Australia with 2889 twin pairs aged between 32 and 43 years. The study found that participants who were classed as a pathological gambler had a 49% chance that their twin was also.

The study suggested that genetic influences may be more important than shared environmental influences in the development of gambling disorders. Each twin had been asked if they had the same friends growing up, shared classes in primary and high school and if they dressed alike when they were between 6 and 13 years. The twins were also asked how often they saw or contacted each other as adults so that the researchers could then assess how similar their adult environment was. The researchers concluded that there was an increased likelihood for a twin to have a gambling problem if their sibling also had a gambling problem but it was due to genetic factors and not environmental factors.

These findings indicate that while genetic predisposition exists, it is likely to be a contributing factor rather than being the sole cause.

- *Just because someone is predisposed genetically to gambling disorders does not mean they will become a problem or compulsive gambler.*

- *Like most illnesses that you may be genetically predisposed to it can be treated and managed.*

- *It also does not mean as a compulsive gambler you will pass on any genetic predispositions to your children*.

Environment.

The environment that you grow up in, or currently find yourself living in has a large impact on developing a gambling problem, for example when gambling is a big part of your family life growing up with a close family member being actively and openly involved with gambling. If you then go one to develop a gambling problem it can be confused with being hereditary. However rather than a genetic reason, it could simply be environmental because it was something you have been exposed to growing up so have gone on to engage in gambling activities almost naturally.

Or another environmental factor could be your friends and work colleagues in everyday life being engaged with gambling and it often being a focus of conversation and social activities. For example many of your peers may be engaged in gambling activities such as sports betting, social games of poker or have an interest in horse racing for example. It is often a source of conversation down the pub or in the workplace, the latest bets, and the latest wins (people seldom discuss their latest loss) and all that chatter makes it hard to not join in. Its human nature to go with the flow and join in with others so it is easy to be drawn into gambling in these scenarios.

Another example of environment being a contributing factor to developing gambling problems is living in a disadvantaged area. There have been several studies carried out proving that people living in poorer neighbourhoods were more likely to report higher frequencies of gambling behaviours and gambling problems than those who lived in more affluent areas. In the UK this is can be seen by walking down the High Street of towns that are struggling economically. How many shops, restaurants and pubs are closed - yet it seems like there is a bookmakers or arcade almost every other building? Unfortunately, people see gambling as a potential easy way to make money or desperately hope to get that big win to solve their financial problems and are willing to risk what little they have to achieve this. The bookmakers are only too happy to take advantage of this and put a lot of effort into promoting the idea of how a big win will change your life for the better and end all your problems, all while rubbing their greedy little hands together in glee.

- *If you have a gambling problem and have decided to stop, think about potentially harmful environments to be avoided.*

- *If people in your company are having conversations about gambling such as the latest football results or horse racing you can always change the subject or even just walk away, especially if in the workplace. If with friends and they know you have stopped gambling ask them not to talk about these things.*

- *If you are supporting someone who is struggling with gambling be mindful of the environment and topics of conversations you find yourself together in.*

Cognitive distortions.

Cognitive distortions, also known as Mind Traps, are ways in which our minds convince us of something that is true when in fact it is not. This is usually to reinforce negative thoughts, feelings, and actions by telling ourselves things that sound rational and accurate to justify them. Cognitive distortions do not just apply to problem and compulsive gamblers, they apply to most people in some form or another. Our own brains are very good at misleading us and can cause problems with anxiety, relationships, and careers, generally holding us back from achieving things in life. One example is Labelling which is when people reduce themselves or others to singular negative characteristic such as loser. Mental filtering is another when people ignore the positive things in their life and focus on the negative. Mind reading, assuming you know what other people are thinking about you or a situation and that it is negative without ever simply asking.

Some of the typical irrational beliefs or cognitive distortions that problem or compulsive gamblers specifically experience, including myself in the past, are as follows:

The Illusion of Control, when you believe you have some control over the events you are gambling upon. That you have some incredible system which is going to surely make you a fortune. I spent hours and hours going through years of horse racing stats and data searching for a fool proof system to make me money. And eventually I found a few instances where certain sets of data and conditions provided a profitable series of previous winners. But it was not really a system, it was just reading the data in a way that was favourable, it had no bearing on future races. But at the time I thought this meant I was in control and my new system would without doubt make me money which of course it did not. I also had an illusion of being in control when it came to Poker by thinking I was a good player who calculated the odds and made the right plays and could beat those who did not. But the truth was I could not maintain the disciple to play as I should and would end up gambling, playing more hands and for bigger stakes than I should have. I also overestimated my level of skill which is a common affect associated with the illusion of control.

Like the Illusion of Control another dangerous cognitive distortion called **Confirmation Bias.** This is when we draw conclusions which suit our needs and fit with our narrative from random events or outcomes and see evidence which is not there.

Superstition is another form of cognitive distortion. Regarding certain situations or items to be either lucky or unlucky, having a lucky machine or game, wearing a lucky hat, having a lucky day or lucky place to go to gamble. The gambler believes that by following certain rituals, wearing certain items, or gambling on certain machines they can control the wins and losses.

Predictive Control is the perception of predicting the outcome of the game. Making assumptions that certain previous results must mean we can calculate a future gambling outcome. For example how many times I played on a fruit machine under the conviction that it had to pay out soon. Or the typical gamblers fallacy such as watching a roulette wheel stop on black several times in succession and being sure it meant the odds of it being red next were huge and betting accordingly. And I have done this playing roulette, I have watched the ball land on black 15 times before I ran out of money and I only started betting on the 12th spin. That one cost me £1500 even though I only bet on the last 4 spins of that sequence. I started with £100 placed on red to win £100 but then when it lost I foolishly assumed red had to come in soon so bet enough on the next spin to win back what I lost plus the original £100 I was trying to win. So the sequence went:

Spin 12: £100 on red, total wagered £100

Spin 13: £200 on red, total wagered £300

Spin 14: £400 on red, total wagered £700

Spin 15: £800 on red, surely it must come in now, it just must, oh crap, total wagered £1500 and I am skint again.

The crazy the thing is I only started off wanting to win a quick £100 but within 4 spins my bet quickly escalated and I was up to a bet of £800 on the fourth bet. If I had another £1500 available at that moment you can bet, pardon the pun, it was all going on red for the next bet. The insanity of the gambling brain. Of course the previous result has no logical bearing on where the roulette ball would land next. But my gambling brain told me 14 times landing on black the 15th absolutely had to be red. At the time I obviously blamed the online casino software, shouting at my computer that it was rigged and they had cheated me. But it happens more than you would imagine, in fact there was a case of 26 blacks on a run recorded at Casino de Monte-Carlo in August of 1913 when gamblers lost millions as the run lengthened expecting a red.

Another one is **Selective Recall** or **Selective Memory** of winnings. We all remember the big wins and even the nearly big wins that spur us on to continue gambling. We do not recall in detail the slow monotonous drain on our souls and funds with loss after loss after loss. The gambling establishments make sure they use this one against us extremely effectively. It is no surprise when you think about it that when playing a slot machine, whether online or in a casino, that as each pound, dollar or euro is spent it just slips by uneventfully. But when you get a win, especially a big win or get onto the bonus feature game, that is a different story. It is all loud music, flashing lights, bells, and whistles then, anyone nearby knows you have won. So the win gets imprinted on your memory and even though you will probably walk away with nothing at the end of the day, when you look back on it sometime later the one thing that stands out is that win. When you think about it logically it makes no sense for the gambling establishment to celebrate you winning. Why should they celebrate giving you money? They do it to keep you playing knowing they will take it back and more besides.

Interpretative Bias is the misguided notion that we can be successful if we continue to gamble and we attribute all past losses and failings to external factors beyond our control. In this way we see it that it is not our fault we have not won big yet but if we persevere we are bound too.

There are many other Cognitive Distortions but the most damaging and misguided of them all is the **Inability to Stop** distortion. We believe we cannot stop gambling and are unable to resist the urge to gamble. Well I can tell you that is not true and that you absolutely can stop gambling and resist those urges, and not only that but the more you do the weaker those urges get.

Once you identify these Cognitive Distortions for what they are you can challenge them and change the way you think. I have personally come to understand that it is my own negative thoughts and how I choose to react to things that causes most of my own problems. In the same way other people are being negatively affected by their own thoughts causing them their own problems. For this reason I try not to take it personally if someone behaves in a negative way towards me as it is likely more a reflection on them than me.

- *Cognitive behavioural therapy (CBT) is a successful practice in gambling treatment. CBT teaches people to identify, question, and change their negative thoughts and behaviours related to gambling, and respond to problem behaviours in a more productive way.*

Escapism.

Many gamblers do so as a form of escapism, in other words they take part in gambling activities to distract them from or to escape from negative things in their life. These could be things such as fear, stress, anxiety, and responsibility. This may start out as a harmless distraction for some but can quickly develop into a dependency or addiction. While they are zoned out in front of a slot machine or laptop screen gambling, they are not thinking about their problems in life. The unfortunate thing is that of course the problems are still there when their gambling session ends and chances are that the very act of gambling is likely to have made matters even worse for them. When the realisation and weight of this becomes too much, they feel the need to escape from it, ironically by gambling, and so the spiral downwards continues. For most gamblers they reach a point where there seems no way out and even though they know gambling is compounding their problems they cannot stop and so descend into despair.

Self-sabotage.

Many gamblers, when trapped in the deep despair of their gambling addiction, will gamble as a way of committing self-sabotage or self-destruction because despite the pain they are in caused by gambling, they begin to believe they deserve it so inflict more. It is a special kind of madness which I too have experienced. I believed I was a despicable person when in actual fact I was not, but my gambling addiction had me all messed up so even though gambling was the root cause of my pain I believed I deserved it and continued to punish myself. In those moments there was absolutely no joy whatsoever in the activity of gambling, it was purely all about how much I hated myself and with every press of the slot machine button and every pound spent that thought was reinforced. I hate myself. I deserve this pain. I am a scumbag.

Of course this was not true and not justified but at the time it seemed so. I do not believe these things any longer thanks to my recovery. However, very occasionally, when I look myself in the eyes in the mirror, a sudden, venomous thought flashes across my mind from nowhere.

"You Scumbag".

When it happens I logically challenge that thought, as I try to do with any negative thoughts, and I see that it is not true but obviously the darker, deeper parts of my psych are trying to cling on to that belief. Part of my recovery is working on bringing light to the darker side of my psych through continuing to develop myself and become a better person.

Cross addictions.

People who are struggling or recovering from one type of addiction such as drug or alcohol sometimes find they transpose their addictive traits to another focus such as gambling. This is known as cross addiction or addiction transfer and can occur many years even after recovery from an earlier addiction. As previously stated our overactive reward system is easily triggered by addictive behaviours causing a release of dopamine and if left unchecked another addiction can form. People with a previous drug or alcohol addiction, whilst more likely to develop a cross addiction, are also best placed to recognise the warning signs and hopefully can react accordingly.

Solution to financial problems.

As mentioned briefly in the Environmental section, people with financial needs or difficulties often see winning money as a quick way out or a solution to their financial problems. If only they could win an extra £500 a month that would really help and how difficult could it be, especially if they are smart about it. When this really becomes a problem and a way into long term gambling addiction is when they have some success early on. If they lost their money straight away they would probably soon realise it was a bad idea and not the answer they were looking for. However, if they win early on they think that it is. Many gamblers have a big win or a few smaller wins early on in their gambling life and that is what really hooks them. They believe, despite subsequent losses, that their early wins mean that they can win again, but now they have the added pressure of not only trying to win the extra £500 they needed but also whatever they have now lost.

But the truth is that now they have started down this path, even if they do win, no amount will be enough. Once the gambling addiction takes hold they will not be able to stop even if they won the set amount they were aiming for. They will simply convince themselves that the smart thing to do now is carry on and win more. After all why stop at what you need for this month when you can win what you need for next month too. No gambling addict has ever won enough, the truth is after a while it is not about the money, it is just about needing to gamble.

6. GAMBLING RELATED HARM

T he "Gambling related harm" report from the UK House of Commons, 18 March 2019, in connection with the Local Government Guidance, highlights several issues around problem gambling.

Gambling related harm does not just affect the person gambling, it affects their colleagues and families as well. It is estimated that for every problem gambler there are a further six to ten people directly affected also. Gambling related harm has a broader stroke than most people would consider and includes financial hardship, crime, mental health problems, relationship breakdown, domestic violence, self-harm, and suicide.

It is estimated that as many as 2 million people in the UK are affected by gambling harm.

Financial harm.

The most obvious gambling harm people will think of is financial harm. When a gambler stops or reduces spending money on essential things such as groceries, clothing, medicine, and general health, rent or mortgage payments then this will cause harm to both themselves and their family. Often things of value may be sold to fund gambling causing adverse effects to their general lifestyle. This is further compounded by increasing levels of debt to fund the gambling addiction leaving the gambler and their loved ones often in financial difficulties for many years. In worse case scenarios gamblers lose the family home causing huge amounts of anguish to their spouse and children. Their credit is ruined and can take several years to rebuild once debts are finally paid off. The financial harm you can cause as a gambling addict is unrivalled by any other addiction. As an alcoholic there is only so much money you can spend on booze before you pass out. As a drug addict you can spend considerably more than an alcoholic but it still has its limits as even a serious cocaine addict can only do so much in a night. A compulsive gambler can spend their entire life savings on one spin of a wheel.

The financial harm caused by gambling does not just sit with the gambler and his family and friends though. There is a wider cost to gambling for the public such as children's services, financial aid and support, housing, policing, medical services, and treatments to name a few. A report funded by GambleAware in December 2016 by the Institute for Public Policy Research (IPPR) published research on the cost of gambling-related harm to Great Britain. The report estimated that the direct cost of problem gamblers to the public purse was between £260 million and £1.2 billion per year. While this is a huge difference from lower to higher estimate even at the lower it is a huge amount of money spent each year due to problem gambling in Great Britain alone.

In comparison the total gross gambling yield (GGY) for the industry in Great Britain, or in other words what they made, was £14.2bn in the year April 2019 to March 2020. – more than enough to foot the bill if the Gambling Industry truly believed it had a care of duty to its customers and general public.

All gambling businesses licensed in the UK by the Gambling Commission are required to contribute towards Research, Education and Treatment (RET) to minimise gambling harms as a condition of their license to allow them to operate. The amount is not set but is in the range of between 0.1% and 1% of their Gross Gambling Yield. Even if all the UK Gambling Industry contributed 1% to help minimise gambling harm it still falls woefully short of what is needed.

The UK Betting and Gaming Council's five largest members confirmed that they would spend £100 million pounds over 5 years improving treatment services for problem gamblers in June 2020. They announced that this would be by way of providing funds to the charity GambleAware who would be the main commissioning agent for ensuring funds reach people who require counselling and treatment. The five operators also pledged to increase the amount they spend on research, education, and treatment (RET) services from 0.1%to 0.25% of their annual revenue in 2020, 0.5% in 2021, 0.75% in 2022 and a generous (can you detect my sarcasm) 1% in 2023.

I appreciate that the UK Gambling Industry also generates tax of between £2 and £3 billion a year over the period of 2013 to 2021 and generates about a hundred thousand jobs in the UK which is great. I am not against the Gambling Industry or the benefits it provides for the UK and other countries, but I believe they can and should do a whole lot more to prevent and treat gambling harm.

The UK is not the only country this applies to, it is worldwide with similar figures all over. The Gambling Industry makes huge fortunes, pays what it must in tax according to the tax laws of that country and pays a woefully inadequate amount towards combating the gambling harm they are responsible for.

Employment.

Gamblers are often not exactly model employees as they tend to be spending more time thinking about gambling than working. It is not unusual for gamblers to call in sick to go spend the day gambling somewhere, have extended breaks while gambling, leave early or arrive to work late as they could not drag themselves away from betting. They might also have more sick days than most because of the negative affect gambling has on their mental and physical health. So between the time off work and slacking off when they are there can often lead to disciplinary action with written and final warnings or just a straightforward sacking. Losing their job because of gambling will not only affect their finances but jeopardize relationships with loved ones and keeping their home.

The other side to this might be that their job is running their own business that other people rely upon for employment. If their gambling addiction runs the company into the ground it is not only the loss of their business but the loss of jobs for its employees.

Crime.

It is no surprise really that some Gambling addicts who struggle with impulse control coupled with a desperate need to find funds to gamble with turn to crime. Also Cross Addictions, mental health disorders and difficult life experiences which can all be associated with gamblers can contribute to crime being committed. The longer someone has a gambling disorder and the longer it goes untreated the more chance there is they will turn to crime. And of course the more chance that they will continue to commit crime if they get away with it. For that reason alone there should be more help available to problem gamblers initially to prevent them turning to crime.

Not all crimes will be white collar such as fraud as some might expect, some crimes are more violent and intrusive in nature such as burglary and armed robbery. In my time as a compulsive gambler attending meetings I have met a few prisoners granted attendance from open prison and a few ex-prisoners who have served their time. For the most part they are good people who have made bad choices in life and are working hard to be upstanding citizens. I say the most part, as I have met one person who showed no remorse for their crimes and no intention of stopping gambling. I think he just used the meeting as an excuse to get out of his open prison for a few hours once a week. There are some people in life who are just not very nice and use gambling as an excuse for their actions.

On the other end of the spectrum I have also met a convicted armed robber who robbed the local bookies where he spent all his money, who was genuinely remorseful for his crime and was working hard to become a better person. He was, to all intent and purposes, a very nice chap who had just made a huge mistake while in the grips and insanity of his gambling addiction. I am not condoning his actions or crime but he served his time, was repentant and was working hard to change his life in a positive manner.

While gambling addiction is beginning to be recognised as a serious disorder, it is not yet translating to sentencing for crimes as drug or alcohol addiction would be. It is not commonly considered as a contributing factor to the circumstances leading up to the crime and often imprisonment is considered an appropriate sentencing, when in fact, rehabilitation, support, and treatment are what is required. I am not saying there should not be punishment and consequences for crimes committed but prison is not always the answer. Gambling is rife in prisons all around the world despite the fact it is prohibited, it is often overlooked by the prison authorities who are already over stretched as they concentrate on other adverse activities. Prison populations all around the world have a much higher proportion of problem and compulsive gamblers than general society with up to a third of prisoners admitting to having a gambling problem in some studies. While gambling is a huge problem in prisons there is very little currently being offered in way of support or treatment. This only escalates the problems caused with the connection of crime and gambling and is not an effective way of rehabilitating the offender. It is also not a cost effective solution to the problem either when support and treatment of the gambling addiction has been overlooked or not available.

Mental Health.

Mental health problems and gambling problems go hand in hand unfortunately. If someone develops a gambling problem they are likely to see their mental health deteriorate to some degree and often to a severe level. Anxiety, stress, depression, and general feelings of low self-worth are all common. I myself have suffered with Anxiety for as long as I have been a compulsive gambler and still do even though it has been many years since my last bet. In fact I believe my anxiety started all the way back at School and figures of authority such as Bosses, Directors and Teachers have always played into my anxiety. There was a period of about 6 months shortly after my son was born when I did not leave the house unless absolutely necessary because of my anxiety and when I had to, it was very traumatic. The thought of having to leave the safety of the house filled me with dread.

I remember one of my rare trips out during this time was once going to a florist to buy some flowers for my wife, presumably for her birthday or Valentines. The whole experience was such an ordeal that when the florist handed me my change I dropped it in a blind panic and just left it on the floor, ran out the door shouting behind me, "Keep the change".

I was contracting at the time and I was generally only working one shift at the weekend because there was not much work available so I did not have to go out too much. I have since had time to reflect on this period in my life and it is no surprise really my anxiety was heightened. I had the new responsibility of being a father for the first time which of course can be a very anxious time for most. However I was already suffering with anxiety, I now had less money, my gambling was continuing despite my fear of leaving the house thanks to the wonders of online casinos and poker rooms so my debts were continuing to mount. Moreover I had the added responsibility of being a financial provider for my baby boy and our new family and insanely, at the time, I thought online Poker was the way to do this.

Fortunately I have been able to learn how to control my anxiety for the most part through coping mechanisms and strategies along with recognising likely anxiety inducing situations and preparing myself well for them. Overall I do not like to avoid them unless absolutely necessary as I believe once you start backing away from such situations you will always back away from them and things get worse. If you avoid a situation because it will make you anxious then what happens is subconsciously you are confirming that it was the right thing to do and giving your anxiety credence. As hard as it is I find it better to face them if possible, get through them and then confirm to myself that I have survived and nothing terrible happened. In this way I am slowly training my overactive Amygdala which is responsible for reacting to situations by releasing stress hormones and triggering my fight or flight reactions to chill the hell out.

My anxiety since stopping gambling is considerably better and I believe my recovery from gambling addiction has also played a major part in my recovery from anxiety. I am not sure my anxiety will ever completely go away and I have accepted that it is part of me and have learned how to live with it. I also take it as a positive as it has taught me to be more understanding and have more empathy towards other people. You never know what someone is going through or what personal battle they are currently fighting and I know through experience despite what it looks like outwardly, they may be going through hell.

The flip side to gambling causing mental health problems is that if you have a mental health problem already, you're more at risk of developing a harmful gambling habit. If you are depressed, anxious, or stressed you may gamble to try to feel better about yourself or find some enjoyment. Even more likely you might begin gambling as a distraction, classic escapism, but because your mental health is not as robust as it could be you find yourself susceptible to developing a gambling problem.

If you are struggling with mental health challenges or if you know someone who is, please do not suffer in silence. There is a much greater awareness now around these things and people now accept that mental health is as important as physical health. There are numerous mental health charities who can help which can be found online. You can call the Samaritans day or night if you need to talk to someone right away. You can make an appointment with your doctor and speak to them in confidence. Some places of employment have confidential services for their employees who can offer counselling for free. There are things like guided meditation which I have found extremely helpful in the past which you can access for free online. And lots of self-help books out there which are great, especially the audio versions if you have a decent commute time available each day. I have a 45 minute commute each morning and evening which to me is an hour and a half each day I can use to listen to audio books and podcasts to help improve my wellbeing and knowledge.

Suicide.

Of all addictions, gambling has the highest suicide rate. I think that shows just how complete and utterly gambling can destroy lives. Maybe it is because of how swiftly it can ruin a life from a financial point of view, thinking there is no way to repay the debts built up and the shame and guilt of how that invariably affects loved ones too. Maybe it is the general lack of understanding and support available for gambling addicts as opposed to say drug and alcohol addictions. Maybe it is the isolation and loneliness of a gambling addiction as you slowly but surely annihilate all relationships with family and friends as you withdraw from them and into the addiction, especially once all financial bridges are burnt. Ultimately when faced with the crushing reality and consequences of their actions many gamblers suffer such low self-esteem and a feeling of hopelessness that suicide seems like the only way.

Most of the people I have personally met in G.A have had suicidal thoughts in the past or even attempted suicide. Some of those people I have not seen in a room for a long time, but people come and go and that is not unusual and due to the anonymity aspect, it is hard to keep track. However, there are one or two people who stand out in my mind and I sometimes wonder if they are still with us. I hope they are.

GamblingWithLives.org is an independent charity set up in the U.K by the families and friends of young people who have taken their own lives as a direct result of gambling. These deaths were not always the result of huge gambling debts as one might think but often the emotional and psychological damage gambling causes. In a lot of cases gambling related suicides come unexpectedly with no warning, most likely due to the secretive nature and lack of visible signs of the addiction.

Research shows that there are likely to be between 250 and 650 gambling related suicides in the UK alone each year. In 2020 there were 6211 suicides recorded in the U.K meaning potentially more than 10 percent of these deaths could be attributed to gambling related causes.

And the trend is tragically the same the world over. Australia is estimated to have 400 gambling related suicides each year and in 2020 there were 3139 suicides total meaning nearly 13% could be attributed to gambling related causes. A study in Hong Kong completed in 2010 found that 11% of suicides were gambling related and another Swedish study in 2018 found that the suicide rate of people with a gambling disorder is 15 times that of the general population.

Anyone in the UK who is struggling to cope and has thoughts of suicide can text 'SHOUT' to 85258 anonymously, confidentially and exchange text messages with a trained volunteer any time of the day or night.

You can also call Samaritans on 116 123, day or night, 24/7, 7 days a week for FREE.

Anyone else outside of the U.K please do an internet search to find someone to talk to or message as there will be similar organisations available to you too. You will be able to speak to someone in confidence about your thoughts and situation and they will be able to advise and signpost you to help. And you do deserve the help, you are worthy, despite how hopeless things may seem at times with the right help you can get your life back on track again. Please reach out, there are people who care.

7. GAMBLING AND CHILDREN

As I explained at the beginning of the book I started gambling very early on in my life and I was a problem gambler by the age of 11 or 12. I am not unique in this though by any means.

There is evidence to show that people who gamble early on in life as children are four times more likely to develop problems with gambling later. The most common forms of gambling for children traditionally have been playing fruit machines which are easily accessed in arcades typically found at holiday resorts but private bets, lotto and scratch cards are also popular with children.

One of the biggest reasons this is such a problem is because a child's brain is not developed sufficiently to be able to make good decisions about gambling. As previously mentioned the brains reward system is the main driving force behind gambling and unfortunately that develops at a much younger age than the prefrontal cortex which affects how we make decisions, control our impulses, and set goals. Because our prefrontal cortex is underdeveloped as children we are subject to poor decision-making and judgment. In fact our brains are not fully developed until we reach our early twenty's so in my case, for example, I had at that point been gambling for half my life. So it is easy to see how this allows problem gambling to take a hold early on in life and become ingrained into a person's behaviours, habits, and mindset. Essentially it means problem or compulsive gamblers like me literally must break the habit of a lifetime and begin rewiring our brains to undo a lifetimes way of thinking and behaving. Fortunately this is possible to do and I have been successful in doing just that myself. As anyone can thanks to our wonderful brains and their capability to change through Neuroplasticity as mentioned in an earlier chapter.

However, the ideal thing is to stop children who are gambling developing into problem or compulsive gamblers in the first place.

According to the Gambling Commissions 2018 report on Children and Gambling they estimate that approximately 450000 children aged 11 to 16 gambles in any given week in the U.K. That equates to 14% of children have gambled in the past week compared to other potential harmful activities, 13% have drunk alcohol, 4% have smoked and 2% have taken illegal drugs. The report estimates that there are somewhere in the region of 55000 children in the U.K who are already problem gamblers. It also shows that only 19% of parents set strict rules about gambling and shockingly in the case of scratch card or buying lottery tickets, 58% of the time the parent or guardian was with the child. It is not that most parents are irresponsible in my opinion, it is just that most people do not realise the potential harm that gambling can cause especially when starting so early in life.

Arcades in the U.K are different than they used to be with less of the video games that used to be in there when I was a child. Street fighter, Pac-man, Ghosts n Goblins, Super Mario Bros and Outrun are lost to mists of time and you will not find many games like that anymore. Most of the games are now all about trying to win tickets which spew out the front of the machine and if you collect a few thousand you can trade them in for a crappy toy. Children are encouraged to hit the jackpot of 500 tickets on the game they are playing. To me this is essentially encouraging children to gamble, hoping to win tickets to trade for prizes instead of just playing games for the joy of seeing if you can get your name on the leader board.

Already with technology being what it is there are more ways for children to gamble than even just a few short years ago due to a frighteningly rapid spreading phenomena called Skin gambling which is largely unregulated and unlicensed.

In the video gaming world, a "skin" is a virtual item that can be won or purchased within the game. They are purely aesthetic - they don't increase the players abilities or affect the outcome of the game in any way. It could be something to customise or decorate weaponry, spells, coins, equipment, or items of clothing to change appearances within the game. These items have become extremely popular in the gaming world, and as such, have in turn amassed value.

Skins were made popular in a video game called Counter Strike: Global Offensive (CS:GO) in 2012 which is owned by the US-based Valve Corporation. Valve also developed the Steam platform, which lets players buy, sell, or trade their personal skin collections for real or virtual currency. This has allowed skins to have value based upon popularity and availability meaning skins have themselves become a virtual online currency.

The popularity of games like CS:GO has given rise to esports, a form of competitive gaming played and watched by millions worldwide. Interest has grown in betting on major Esport matches and third party websites initially set up for trading skins started allowing gamers to bet on the outcome of the Esport matches. This quickly moved on to allowing betting skins on roulette, coin tosses, wheels of fortune and slots. While you cannot withdraw money from Steam or the third-party gambling sites, additional sites have emerged allowing users to exchange skins for cash – or essentially cash in their chips. Some skins are worth tens of thousands of pounds, dollars, or euros. Very few of these third-party gambling sites use age verification or operate under any gambling licensing or regulatory bodies.

Another form of gambling with skins is the practice of buying Loot Boxes in games with real money and hoping it contains skins worth more than you paid for the Loot Box. Sometimes this is the case but often you get skins worth less or duplicates instead. Often there is no real information on what the chances are of getting the high valued items and children are gambling without any real knowledge of the chance of success.

Technology is ever evolving and it will always be the younger generation who are ahead of the curve while parents get left behind. It has always been this way; I remember having to set up the VHS recorder for my parents who did not know how to work it. Most children these days would not even know what one is. Even now trying to explain to my mum in her 70's how her smartphone works is challenging. But I am no different in trying to understand all the things my teenage son talks to me about in relation to his Xbox games. In a world where parents are unlikely to fully understand the games their children are playing and what is involved it is easy to see how this new type of gambling can go unnoticed. And you know what, in most cases it will not lead to a problem for people but in some cases it absolutely will and likely lead onto other traditional forms of gambling. So if you can drag your grumpy teenager away from the games console for a short while its worth just having a conversation with them about this kind of stuff and the dangers involved.

Seriously though, I believe all parents should have an honest chat with their kids about gambling and the potential harm it can cause. Pick the right moment when there is not much going on, after a show has finished on TV, while out taking a leisurely stroll, on a drive somewhere, or just working on a job together around the house. Tailor the conversation to them, if they like gaming talk about loot boxes and skins, if they like sports talk about sports betting. Whatever you talk about keep it short and relaxed, a long winded talk will just have them tune out and best to have a couple of short conversations that are listened to than a long one forgotten. And remember listening is a two way street, actively listening to what they say is vital and will encourage them to talk more openly.

8. THE ODDS ARE NEVER IN YOUR FAVOUR

T he vast majority of people know in their heart of hearts that you cannot win when it comes to gambling. On the off chance you are one of the people struggling with the Illusion of Control, as I used to, and many compulsive gamblers do, please take in the stark truth of this next chapter. The odds are never in your favour and you cannot win.

As soon as you place a bet you have lost the only advantage you ever had over bookies, casinos, or any gambling establishments because the only way not to lose is not to bet. Occasionally you hear of someone who has won the first time they bet and walks away and never to bets again. The bookies and casinos are fine with that because they know that rarely ever happens in real life. Usually, even if someone wins in their first experiences with gambling, they figure why not do it again. as they have nothing to lose but the previous winnings and they might win again, why not, it was easy last time. But the longer you play the more you lose and its simple mathematics, not luck or skill, that determine this thanks to a thing called the Law of Large Numbers.

All the odds of any gambling activity are stacked against the gambler and are in favour of the casino. They are a business after all and their business is taking your money, they would not operate for long if they could not guarantee this. What is commonly known as the House Edge in casinos is the way they ensure this. Roulette for example is over 5% in their favour, even betting on red or black is not 50/50 as some people like to think because of the zero and double zero. Slots can be up to 15% in the casinos favour. Scratch cards are about 30% in their favour. Blackjack is the lowest at 2% or 0.5% if you know how to play the perfect strategy, but few people do and even less manage to stick to it, regardless, you will still lose overall. Whatever the casino game, the margin or house edge, is always there to varying degrees and always in their favour.

The Law of Large numbers basically states that the more you play the more the results will reflect the actual odds and percentages. Take roulette, as mentioned before it has over a 5% margin built into the casinos favour. So out of every £100 spent you lose £5 which you might think is not too bad but it all comes down to how long you play for and the casinos want you playing for a long time and placing bets in quick succession. Say a roulette table plays on average of 50 spins in an hour in a real casino, online will be much quicker. If you sit down with £100 and are playing level stakes at £5 a spin you are losing £10 or £15 per hour so over 4 hours play an actual loss of about £50, half of your money. Let's be honest, how many gamblers will patiently sit there just betting £5 on each spin? Once you factor in chasing losses and increasing the level of bets the more the casino will take from you overall.

Bookies are exactly the same when taking your bets on any sporting event, be it a multiple runner or just a two possible outcome event. The odds are of course calculated in their favour every time, so regardless of the outcome they win. For example, in a straightforward two outcome event such as which team will win the coin toss. Despite the fact it is a 50/50 outcome each team will have odds of 10/11 meaning that even if you placed £100 on team A and someone else puts £100 on team B whichever one wins the bookie only pays out £91 plus the initial stake returned. So regardless which team wins for every £200 staked they are guaranteed £9 profit if the book is balanced. (If equal bets are placed on both teams).

For any two outcome betting event the margin is usually 2% to 5% in the bookies favour but once you start betting on multiple outcome events such as horse racing the margins grow to between 10% and 20% meaning even greater profits for them and losses for you. The markets change and odds go up and down but that is driven by the bookies trying to balance their books and maintain those margins in their favour which of course they are very good at doing. So if a favourite gets more money on it that they like they will reduce the odds making it less attractive while increasing the odds on another selection which has not had as much money wagered on it making it more attractive. This helps to keep the books balanced ensuring which ever selection is successful they get their profit.

You cannot beat the bookies or casinos and the longer you try the more you play into their hands and continue to reduce the chance of winning. Of course they love to welcome you to try. That is why casinos offer comps like free drinks and hotel rooms to keep you there longer. And all the rumours you hear about casinos being designed in such a way as to keep you gambling are true. Some have no windows or clocks so you do not realise how long you are there. All the glitter and excitement making you think that you have a chance at being the one to win it all. They are set up like labyrinthine with walls of slot machines meaning you have to take many twists and turns to get to where you want to be. The longer it takes and the more slot machines you have to pass the more chance one will catch your eye and you will either sit down or go back to it. Also the shorter line of sight encourages you to explore more and see what is around the corner, again exposing you to more slot machines. The reduced line of sight also plays into the solitary nature of the compulsive gambler as they feel closed in away from prying eyes. They employ various other methods to stimulate our senses such as the sound of coins paying out when they no longer actually pay out coins, flashing lights, exciting music, colourful settings, and even pleasant smells all to trigger the desire to gamble.

The bookies, arcades and online casinos are no different in their welcoming nature of wanting to entice us to gamble. They all offer comps, free bets, bonuses, and all wrapped up in advertising based on happy smiley people winning lots of money. Whatever it takes to get you gamble and keep gambling because the more you do and the longer you do it for the more money they take from you.

So what are the actual odds of you winning?

- **Hitting Blackjack (bizarrely) is 21/1 (not forgetting if the dealer also gets Blackjack it is a push meaning you get your stake back so you neither win nor lose).**

- **Winning £5 on a scratch card is 900/1 (on a £1 play £100,000 jackpot card).**

- **Winning the Jackpot on a 3 reel slot machine with 20 positions per reel is 8000/1 (video or virtual slot can have up to 256 symbol positions so odds can be 16,777,216/1)**

- **Winning £20 on a scratch card is 14,884/1 (on a £1 play £100,000 jackpot card).**

- **Getting a royal flush in Texas Hold 'em Poker is 30,939/1**

- **Winning the Jackpot on a 4 reel slot machine with 20 positions per reel is 160,000/1**

- **Winning £50 on a scratch card is 179,803/1 (on a £1 play £100,000 jackpot card).**

- **Getting a royal flush in 5 card Poker is 649,739/1**

- **Winning £1000 on a scratch card is 4,270,320/1 (on a £1 play £100,000 jackpot card).**

- **Winning £100,000 Jackpot on a scratch card is 5,693,760/1 (on a £1 play £100,000 jackpot card).**

- **Winning the Jackpot on a 6 number lottery with 49 balls is 13,983,816/1**

- **Winning the Jackpot on a 6 number lottery with 59 balls is 45,057,474/1**

So you can see the odds are clearly not in your favour, nowhere near.

You cannot Win. You cannot Win. You……..Can……..Not………Win.

9. GUILT OF A GAMBLER

G ambling addiction can make a person dishonest, untrustworthy, despicable, selfish, devious, conniving, hurtful, angry and a compulsive liar as well as compulsive gambler. So it is no surprise that with gambling comes guilt, especially when having stopped and beginning to gain control again.

But you should not feel guilt or shame for becoming addicted to gambling in the first place. The gambling industry spend a huge amount of time, energy, and money employing some very clever people to make their slot machines, advertisements, online games, and everything to do with their business as addictive as possible. That is the whole purpose of their business, to get you to become addicted and take your money. So you became addicted to something that is designed to be addictive, that's hardly your fault is it?

Guilt is of no use to the recovery of a gambler but it is unavoidable in the early days as your mind begins to clear and you start to get back in touch with your emotions and feelings. In a way it is a good thing to initially feel guilty because it shows you are a decent human being who cares. But you need to move past the guilt as all it will do is make you feel awful about yourself and this is an easy path back to gambling. You cannot be free from gambling while clinging onto guilt. You must remember that you are not a bad person you have just been a person gripped by a gambling addiction that made you do a lot of bad things. I am not saying you should just forget how you used to be or how many people you have hurt along the way when addicted to gambling. It is a useful tool in your recovery to look back at what kind of person you used to be and know that you do not want to go back there again. Beyond that it serves no purpose to dwell on the past, make amends where you can unless to do so will cause more harm but then move on.

I am all too aware it is easier said than done and although I strongly believe guilt serves no purpose there are still some things I look back on and struggle not to feel guilt and shame about. I used to feel guilty about not being the best father I could be and always say my biggest regret is not the money spent but the time lost with my family. I have focused on working at being the best father I can be but it is still a work in progress and always will be but I am confident I am a good Dad. I will still well up with tears though when talking about it in group because it is hard to ignore those wasted years. A but I know I must forgive myself and I am working on it.

I felt guilty for a long time after I stopped gambling about how I had betrayed a friend years ago financially and he never knew. I could not get away from the fact that I had to come clean with him if I was going to move on and pay him what was owed, but not just that, he was my friend and he deserved better from me, he deserved the truth. I stressed about it for such a long time. I thought he would probably forgive me because he is such a nice guy but perhaps not, but even so, surely he would hold it against me a little and our friendship would never be the same again. How could he not? I was just going to have to take whatever consequences came.

So eventually I arranged to go see him and confess what I had done all those years ago. I told him I was a compulsive gambler and had been for many years, not that he did not already know this I guess but I had never admitted it before. I offered him the money I owed, told him how sorry I was and asked if he could ever forgive me. Not only did he forgive me but he refused to take the money telling me it was OK and not to worry about something I had done years ago when I was a different person. I am really very fortunate to have a small handful of friends in my life who are incredible and generous and I do not deserve them but I am extremely grateful. He is one of them and nothing changed between us except that I love him even more as a friend. I also accept that not everyone would react as he did and not everyone will have such a positive result to coming clean and be granted forgiveness.

The other thing from my past which I felt guilty about for the longest time was betraying someone I loved very much but who unfortunately is no longer here and will never be able to forgive me. When I was younger I had a Great Auntie Rose who was an incredible woman whom I loved immensely. She was a wonderfully kind woman with a fantastically wicked sense of humour, very loving and a proud Liverpudlian who I thought the world of growing up. She lived in the middle of a row of terraced houses in Fazakerley, Liverpool, the kind with a large stone doorstep at the front of the house that she kept scrubbed clean. She was very house proud and looking back I do not believe she had a lot or was well off but what she did have she looked after. She was generous also, she always made sure we were well fed whenever we visited and she would always slip me a couple of quid as I left.

When I was in my late teens she got Cancer, I do not remember what type exactly but I do remember how ill it made her. I remember going to see her in hospital with my parents and I was shocked at how much weight she had lost. She was never a big woman; in fact she was always slender in appearance but as I looked at her while she lay in that hospital bed it struck me that she now looked skeletal. She turned to look at me after a moment and I hope it was long enough for me to hide the look of shock from my face. She beamed a smile at me and jovially stated how great she looked having lost some weight. I told her I preferred my women with a little meat on them and maybe she should try eating some of her meals. I could tell she was in pain and obviously not well but she still did her best to look presentable with her hair brushed and bedding smoothed flat either side of her. As always she tried to make sure we had something to eat offering biscuits or sweets from her bedside table. She joked and chatted and acted as though everything was fine all the time we sat with her even though it obviously was not. A few days later I was supposed to go back to the hospital with my parents and see her again. Instead of heading home on the train to meet them after work to then drive up to the hospital I called my parents to say I was stuck on a fault at work and was going to be hours yet and unfortunately would not be able to make it home to go visiting. I made this phone call as I was walking across the road to the arcade outside Liverpool Lime Street. I never got the chance to go and see her again. The desire to gamble was so strong that I chose to do that and leave someone I loved very much lie dying in a hospital bed. I see now that it was a classic case of escapism too, I did not want to deal with my Auntie Rose dying so chose to go the arcade. I am also not saying that is any kind of excuse I am just saying honestly that it was part of the reason I gambled that day. It is difficult to shake that kind of guilt off even though its over 25 years ago but I believe my Auntie Rose would have forgiven me and I must forgive myself too.

There is no justice in living with guilt. The true sense of justice would be to accept the responsibility for a wrongdoing, accept the consequence, accept the potential punishment, and then move on. When living in guilt you are constantly punishing yourself for the same offense time and time again.

Holding on to guilt keeps you trapped in the past and keeps you tied to the person you once were and as you need to change as a person you need to let go to move on. You cannot move forward and take those important steps along the road of recovery with one foot stuck in the past. You should not spend too much time thinking about the future either as who knows what will happen. By living in the present and doing your very best right now you are very likely to create a fantastic future.

So how do you move on and begin to live your life without guilt?

Well firstly you must accept that you cannot be a truly awful person because people who do not care do not feel guilt. So logically you can see straightaway you are not as bad as you think you are.

If you can make amends then do so. If nothing else a heartfelt apology might go a long way towards re-building bridges but also remember the people you have hurt might need a little time before forgiving you. They have no doubt heard it all before and you will have to allow them the time to realise this time is different and to see the changes in you.

Accept that the gambling addiction is to blame for the majority of the bad things you have done. It is not your fault, you are not to blame, your addiction is. That is not to say that you are not responsible to sort out the problems you now have because of your addiction. It is certainly no one else's responsibility but your own but that does not mean you have to do it alone, use the many resources available to you.

10. THE BEST TIME TO STOP GAMBLING

When is the best time to stop gambling? Now. Now is the best time to stop gambling. Right now. Not tomorrow or next week or when you have done this or done that. You can stop right now; you have no reason to wait.

Once you begin making dates in the future to quit all you are doing is making excuses not to stop gambling. You may have a particular sporting event that you normally have a bet on so want to wait until after then. Well guess what, there will always be another sporting event after that too. You might have arranged to go the races with some friends soon. Perhaps you have already paid for the ticket in advance. Well cancel, do not concern yourself with the money you will lose on the ticket. It will be peanuts in comparison to what you could lose gambling not only on the day but between now and then also. If they are good friends you can tell them why and they will support you. Or do not tell them why if you are not yet ready to. They can still go ahead and have their day out, they might miss you but trust me, you are not so special that it will ruin their day if you are not there. You may have a particular date in mind that you feel has some significance like a birthday, anniversary or maybe New Year's Day. All such dates are just another day and there is no better day to stop than today.

And you can stop, believe me you can. Today should be a day to rejoice because you are beginning a new life free from the insidious addiction of gambling.

Most people at some point shortly after they begin their recovery think to themselves, "I can never have a bet again". And it fills them with both fear and sorrow because they have been under the illusion that they need gambling in their life and that they enjoy it or that it brings them comfort. They feel as though they are saying goodbye to a loved one for ever. The reality is that you are saying goodbye to your worst enemy, an evil addiction that is ruining your life. Gambling does not bring you joy or comfort. All it does when you gamble is to quieten the gambling addiction or urge for a short while. It is not joy that you are feeling, you are not smiling from ear to ear with a song in your heart and spring in your step when gambling. It is not real comfort you are feeling, you do not feel really relaxed and content and as though all is right with the world when you are gambling. All you are doing is quietening the urge to gamble for a time so you are under the illusion that you are happy and content. But it will not last, it never does last which is why you must rid yourself of the urge.

- **You are not giving up something that is good when you stop gambling.**

- **You are giving up pain and misery.**

- **You are giving up lies and deceit.**

- **You are giving up a life of mounting debt and financial hardships.**

- **You are giving up the stress and anxiety that gambling creates and the ill health this causes, both physically and mentally, which can potentially lead you to suicide.**

So do not think to yourself with a heavy heart, "I can never have a bet again".

Rejoice and think to yourself, "I am stopping gambling today and I never have to have another bet again. I am no longer going to be a slave to my addiction".

Today is the first day of a better life ahead, it may not be easy but with the right support, motivation and practical measures put in place you can absolutely do it. I gambled for 30 years and was as bad as anyone, lost in my addiction, but I stopped. If I can stop then believe me, you can stop too.

And once you stop gambling and begin your road to recovery you start to get your life back on the right track. You start to get your self-respect back. You start to enjoy being honest with people, especially those you love, and not having to tell lies. You start to regain your emotions instead of feeling dead inside. You start to feel better in yourself, happier and calm now you no longer have to frantically try to keep all the plates spinning. You start to get your finances in order without the added drain on your money that gambling caused. You start to enjoy the simple things in life again and take genuine pleasure from them.

Once you free yourself from the chains and misery of gambling your life becomes so much better and in turns the lives of those you love too. It also means you become better equipped to deal with life's general ups and downs that before we would have used as excuses to gamble.

11. THE INITIAL THREE STEPS TO STOPPING GAMBLING

Honesty.

T he first step is to have an honest conversation with someone. Learn to be honest with yourself and be honest with others. So far you will have been telling numerous lies about your finances and how you spend your time so that you have been able to gamble. You have no doubt lied and been dishonest about many other things too because it is well known that problem gamblers become accomplished liars. It is time for all that to stop and to begin to tell the whole truth about your gambling problems. You need to tell your story to someone, not everyone but someone, and unburden yourself of all the lies and dishonest acts from your past so you can move on. This can be a loved one, close friend or family member, counsellor or therapist, or likeminded people in a support group such as Gamblers' Anonymous.

If you have a significant other then I recommend it should be them, if not then a friend or family member. You may even want to tell a family member or friend first and ask them for some moral support when you do tell your partner. You need to give it some thought as to who the best person is to initially talk to that can offer you the support that you are going to need. By coming clean and being honest with whoever it is you choose, you are also asking for their help as well as forgiveness, which I know is a difficult thing to do but must be done.

I know through experience how hard it is to admit the truth and the difficulties that brings to a relationship but ultimately there is no other choice but to be totally honest with your loved ones when you decide to give up gambling. I know the prospect of admitting the extent of your gambling addition to your loved ones and what that will do to your relationships is extremely frightening. The truth is that if you do not stop gambling it will eventually ruin all relationships you hold dear and in fact probably already has to some extent but it may not be too late to save them. In my experience through G.A., some members have found loved ones are relieved to have been told the truth. They had been aware of the stress and distancing in the relationship but not understood why and had been worrying not knowing what to do. Relationships and trust can usually be rebuilt over time if you are prepared to put the work in and be gamble free and honest. Honesty really is the best policy when you stop gambling and you can absolutely do it.

Now I cannot stress this enough, it is vitally important to get the whole story out there. Do not hold anything back because you are worried about the reaction of the person you are confessing to; how much it is going to hurt them and that they can only take so much. Yes it is a very difficult conversation, probably the most difficult conversation you will ever have in your life. Yes it is extremely painful and upsetting for all involved but here's the thing. If you leave something out, if you do not disclose the full extent of your debt and your loved one finds out later down the line, and they probably will, then the trust and healing you have built up again will be destroyed. They will naturally think if you kept that from them then what else have you not told the truth about? How can they trust that you have you even really stopped gambling? Also anything you keep to yourself such as a debt or a particular gambling habit can be a potential path back to gambling.

Think of it like taking a plaster or a band aid off your arm. You do not want to draw it out and do a little at a time prolonging the pain and discomfort. You want to rip it off in one go and get it over and done with.

Help.

The second step is to seek the help you need and initially form a plan to get you started on the road to recovery. By taking the first step you will have hopefully already started to get some help from the person or persons who you have told your story to. But do not take too long forming a plan, the important thing is to get moving on it, get started and develop your plan as you move along.

There is lots of help out there when you look for it: Gamblers Anonymous, your Doctor, Counsellors and Therapists, CBT, Hypnotism, Debt Management specialist, Legal aid, books, websites, forums, social media groups and loved ones. All these things and more are available to you and the vast majority will not cost you a thing. I recommend you try them all if you can. Different things work for different people with varying levels of success but you will not know what works for you unless you try them. It might be one thing or it might be a combination of methods and resources that you need to help you stop gambling. Some things might be particularly useful at a certain stage of your recovery but can be discarded once they have served their purpose before moving on to the next one.

Even things like Counselling and Hypnotherapy might not work for you initially but sometimes that is more to do with the therapist and not yourself. I have found through experience that you need to find a therapist you connect with and some are better than others. I have a chapter outlining some of the different therapies available later in the book. Gambling addiction is a mighty beast and you should use every weapon at your disposal to slay it.

Become your better self.

The third step is to get your mindset right, decide to become a better person and believe in yourself. Gambling turns us into horrible people but we are not horrible people at heart. The gambling addiction wants you to believe that you are so it can keep its control of you. Once you begin to turn things on its head and you take control of the gambling and not the other way around you can begin to become your better self.

You do, absolutely, need to change as a person. Simply put, being the person you have been so far has not been able to stop gambling so it stands to reason you need to change and for the better. I cannot stress this enough; it is so important you understand this. You need to change as a person and become the best version of yourself possible.

You need to believe in yourself but also in a higher power. You need to believe and accept there is something greater than yourself. Let's be honest, when you are at rock bottom and gambling has you beat it is not too difficult to believe there is a power greater than yourself. Now believing in a higher power does not have to be a religious thing but it can be and that is fine. Equally your higher power that you draw strength and support from might be family or friendship or a group such as Gamblers Anonymous. It might be a general belief in all that is great and good in the world and the universe. Whatever your higher power is you must believe it is going to raise you up and restore you to a happier way of thinking and living.

Believe in yourself. Believe that you deserve to be the best version of yourself and living your best life.

Our thoughts are the only thing that hold us back. Your subconscious controls your thoughts not you. You are simply the thinker of your thoughts. They are not a reflection of your potential best self; they do not define you. Your subconscious operates in the shadows unbeknownst to you and is made up of all your past experiences both good and bad. Our thoughts are our worst enemy at times and we must learn to control them not the other way around.

Once you are aware of your subconscious you can change it by challenging your negative thoughts. Really dig into where they are coming from and what is behind them. Then call them out for what they are, bullshit.

You can be your best self; you do deserve your best life and you can achieve it. Believe in yourself.

12. ROADBLOCKS TO HELP YOU STOP GAMBLING

T here are numerous practical measures you can, and should, put in place in different areas of your life to enable you to stop gambling, or Roadblocks as I like to call them. The two most important and vital aspects of your life you must apply these Roadblocks to first is access to gambling and access to finances.

You should implement into your life all the Roadblocks suggested even if you think they will not apply to you, and any others you can think of too. The more Roadblocks you have in place the better. There are two main reasons for this:

1 - cut off any potential paths back to gambling including paths you have never taken before. For example, excluding yourself from bookmakers even though that is not your preference of choice when gambling. I guarantee in a moment of weakness if bookies are your only possibility you are going to go in and gamble. If you have excluded yourself from all the bookmakers in your local area that you pass daily there is little chance of that happening. Now do not get me wrong, if you decide you want to have a bet then you are going to travel outside of your local area and go find a bookie you are not excluded from. Roadblocks are not infallible, they are as they sound, an obstruction between yourself and having a bet. Simply put, the more roadblocks that you must circumnavigate to have a bet and the longer that takes the more time you have to come to your senses and make the correct decision that you do not want to gamble. You can then do an about turn on the rocky path to ruinous gambling and continue the righteous road to recovery.

2- prove you are determined to beat gambling and that you will no longer be controlled by it. You are proving to loved ones but more importantly yourself that you are taking this serious and willing to do what it takes to recover from your gambling addiction. You are taking decisive measures and mean business. Your confidence and self-belief will build with every roadblock you put in place that you are able to stop gambling. You can and will stop gambling and regain control of your life.

Self-Exclusion.

All licensed gambling businesses in Great Britain must have their own self exclusion policy or scheme but in addition to this they must sign up to multi-operator schemes too. This is required to be provided by law as an option by any gambling operators in Great Britain. You can ask the gambling operator to exclude you from gambling with them for a set amount of time usually a minimum of six months to twelve months which can be extended at the end of the term. Once activated you cannot revoke or cancel the exclusion prior to the agreed end date. Other countries should have their own self exclusion schemes and gamblers outside of the UK should do some research, most likely via an internet search, to see what it is they need to do to self-exclude. Another possibility is to take a loved one with you for moral support and walk into the gambling establishment you frequent and demand to be self-excluded.

Self-exclusion is a voluntary agreement between the gambler and the gambling provider and must be entered into freely. This means that it cannot be set up on someone else's behalf such as a loved one who you are concerned about.

Any information shared is kept confidential and is only shared with the participating gambling providers and their central teams and not outside of this.

The ultimate responsibility for sticking to any self-exclusion rests with the person who registers for the self-exclusion agreement. If that person attempts to enter premises to place a bet or gamble they will be considered to have breached the terms and conditions of the agreement and asked to leave. In the case of self-exclusion from online sites, which you can do for five years, you should not be able to open an account.

Betting Shops or Bookmakers.

As already mentioned you can self-exclude from Bookmakers, or betting shops, and not only that you can do it for multiple bookmakers in the UK and NI in one go using the Multi Operator Self Exclusion Scheme. This allows the public to self-exclude centrally with more than one operator with a single call for a period of twelve months, usually in areas where they live, work or even holiday. Any location that they may visit on a regular basis for one reason or another. The scheme works by a person submitting a copy of photographic ID via email or post along with a photo of themselves which is shared with the operators they are self-excluded from to help staff recognise them and intervene if they attempt to place a bet. The number to call to register for Multi Operator Self Exclusion is 0800 294 2060 and more information can be found at www.self-exclusion.co.uk.

Arcades or Adult Gaming Centres (AGCs).

Most but not all Arcades are part of an association called Bacta which runs a Self-Exclusion scheme which can be joined by visiting an AGC or by calling the Bacta Self-Exclusion services on 020 7730 644. You can choose to self-exclude for a period of six or twelve months and can be extended for further periods of six months at a time. Once you self-exclude it will come into force immediately and will not be lifted until the end of the chosen period. At the end of the self-exclusion period you will remain excluded unless contacting the operator in person. If the exclusion is lifted it is subject to a 24 hour cooling off period.

You can exclude from a single premise or self-exclude using their multi operator scheme in which case you will have to provide a photograph of yourself to the operator or allow them to take a photo. You will then sign an agreement outlining the period of self-exclusion and that your photo and details may be shared with other operators so they can exclude you from their premises also.

Bingo.

The Bingo Industry Self-Exclusion scheme is run by the Bingo Association and allows customers to self-exclude from licensed land based bingo premises across Great Britain. The scheme works by a customer completing an application form for self-exclusion and providing a digital image of themselves. The individual will be interviewed by a trained member of staff to ensure they fully understand the consequences of the self-exclusion before the process can be completed. This can all be done in person at a local licensed bingo premises or if they do not wish to enter the premises they can call them to start the process. Details of the scheme and the self-exclusion form needed can be found also at www.Bingo-Association.co.uk and following receipt of the form a member of the

Association will contact the customer usually within two working days to complete the process. You can choose between six and twelve months exclusion and once agreed cannot be terminated early. Once your chosen self-exclusion term is over it remains in place for a further six months unless you complete a Reinstatement Request form. Once a reinstatement request has been received a 24 hour cooling off period will be enforced.

Casinos.

The SENSE, Self-Enrolment National Self Exclusion program, is a scheme that people can sign up to exclude themselves nationally from all land based UK casinos. Exclusion is for a minimum of six months and can only be lifted after that time has passed. The lifting of the self-exclusion can only take place at a casino venue and most casino operators have a policy of interviewing the returning customer before being allowed to gamble again. Enrolment can take place at any casino venue or the form can be downloaded from www.nationalcasinoforum.co.uk and emailed or sent by post to avoid having to enter the casino premises. A recent photograph, a copy of photographic ID and proof of address must also be submitted along with the form.

Online gambling.

GAMSTOP.co.uk is a sign up service which prevents you from using gambling websites or apps run by companies registered in the UK for a period of six months to five years. To sign up you will need to provide email addresses, postcode, and date of birth. Once the duration of exclusion has elapsed it will remain in place until you return to GAMSTOP and ask for it to be removed and go through the relevant process. If you move house or change your last name you must update your details with GAMSTOP.

The service will not stop you getting emails from gambling sites so you will need to unsubscribe yourself. Nor will it mean any funds held in accounts with the gambling sites are automatically returned to you. You would need to contact the companies direct for this.

Gamstop will only help to a point as it can only work with UK registered companies. For other gambling sites there should be an option to self-exclude which you will have to do yourself along with any other sites you feel you might use in the future. Of all the self-exclusion methods online is the one that really is down to yourself to make it work as unlike bricks and mortar gambling venues where you can be physically stopped by staff, there is no such gate keeper online. That is where gambling blocking software comes in to help you further in abstaining from online gambling. Gambling specific software such as GamBan is designed to block gambling websites and should be installed on all devices you own or have access to. There are several to choose from and I would encourage you to do your own research. Some are free and some charge a fee, some are better suited to different operating systems or types of computers while others can be found via an app for smartphones and tablets. Some smartphones and tablets have parental controls which stop access to gambling sites in which case you would need someone else to set your password for you.

Most countries should have their own Self Exclusion schemes and an internet search will soon help you to discover what they are and how to go about it.

Money.

Obviously getting control of your finances is a major part of your recovery from Gambling addiction. There are two elements to this, one is having access to money with which you would use to gamble and the other is looking at handling the debts you have accrued.

Giving over Control to gain Control.

Lots of Gamblers find the best thing to do at the beginning of their recovery is to give total control of their money over to a loved one, family member or friend who they trust. By this I mean total control. They must sit down with the chosen person and have a frank and honest conversation about exactly what money they earn or have access to, how much money they owe and how much money they need on a daily or weekly basis. I cannot stress enough how important it is to have an HONEST conversation. By that I do mean talk about how much debt you are in, do not leave anything out. You have already engaged in a difficult and upsetting conversation about your gambling, most likely hurting the loved ones in your life and ruining their trust in you. It is hard, I know, but you must get it all out on the table in order to start afresh and gain their full support. There is nothing more damaging than having a debt surface further down the line that you held back just as your loved ones are beginning to build their trust in you again. And it is natural to not want to give a full and honest account of your debts because you feel ashamed and you may want to limit the pain you are causing your loved ones but it is important to get it all out there in one go. Remember the band aid analogy, you want to rip it off in one go even though it hurts rather than slowly a bit at a time. Get it all out there and then you can start afresh safe in the knowledge you have nothing to hide. I have seen it before when someone who has been clean from gambling for over six months had gradually built the trust of their wife back up only to have it shattered when his sister mentioned the £5000 he still owed her in front of them. His wife knew nothing of this and thought that if he had not been truthful about the extent of debt he was in, how could she believe he had even stopped gambling and there were not more hidden debts?

The recovering gambler should ideally have their income paid directly into their trusted person's bank account with monthly outgoings paid from there. Then the gambler is essentially given a small daily allowance, the bare minimum they require for day to day expenditures, so that they are not carrying much or any cash at all with them. This does three things, the obvious is that they cannot blow their wages gambling if they do not have access to the money. Secondly their financial commitments such as loans, rent or mortgage payments are being made regularly reducing the risk of further financial ruin. And thirdly it is a huge relief for the gambler not having to worry about if their bills will be paid or how they are going to find more money because they blew the mortgage payment in the bookies. Financial stress, along with any type of stress is a trigger to gamble so removing the responsibility of being in control of money is hugely beneficial to the recovering gambler.

If you are not comfortable or willing to give absolute control of your finances over to someone else the next best thing is to give shared control of your account. If someone can see the detail of your account and how much money is going in, how much is being spent and where it is being spent it helps to keep you honest. It is hard to draw out a large amount of money or make transfers to gambling sites and get away with it when a loved one can see straight away what you are doing. Banking Apps on mobile phones can be set to immediately send a notification of any transaction. It is not as fool proof as the first option of giving up total control, you can still blow a lot of money but not without being discovered. Knowing that you will be found out if you were to spend money gambling is a great deterrent but often not enough to stop the very worse afflicted by this insidious illness which is why I strongly recommend relinquishing your financial control to someone else.

A further scaled down version of shared control still is to hand over your bank card and credit cards to a loved one and ask for them when needed and used in their presence. This is the least preferred as it is the easiest to get around but again it is a roadblock and hopefully the time it takes you to get around it is enough time for you to come to your senses.

In all cases if you have a shared bank account with a spouse or loved one and you do not relinquish control of it then they should take out all their own money and open their own account.

I have never had a joint account with my wife that both our wages got paid into but only because I did not want her to see what I was spending my money on or how much it was. That was all about protecting my gambling addiction and not about protecting her finances. We do have a joint account which is for paying the bills and I automatically transfer a set amount into from my personal account each month but I deliberately do not give that account to much attention or thought.

You may not be fortunate enough to have someone in your life who you can give total or shared control of your finances to but there are still plenty more measures you should put in place. If you are fortunate enough to have help from a loved one you must still put the following measures in place also.

Your bank account and Gambling transactions.

You must inform your bank that you do not want any gambling related transactions to be allowed. More and more banks are getting on board with this but if yours is not then you must change your account to another bank. This is a tremendous roadblock if online gambling is your thing especially coupled with self-exclusion and online blocking software.

Stop carrying large amounts of cash and your cash card.

When you first give up gambling you should avoid carrying any money or anything other than loose change in your day to day routine. If you need more than loose change then plan and only carry what you need and spend it on what you plan to. You should certainly never carry large amounts of money in your pocket, most people's day to day routines do not require that they need hundreds of pounds on them and neither should you. How many times have you nipped out to the shop for a pint of milk and took a wedge of cash with you only to decide to call into the bookies on the way for a minute, come out much later having spent the lot and go home without the milk? It might not be milk but the story is the same for many a gambler. Do not have large stashes of cash around, it is too great a temptation. Leave your money in the bank and only carry small amounts even when you are well on the road to recovery.

Do not carry your cash card around all the time either, leave it at home unless you need it. If you are fortunate to live with someone who is supporting you but you still control your own finances leave it somewhere visible like the mantel piece or kitchen worktop so if you have taken it they will notice. Encourage them to challenge you when they notice it has gone. Talk to your bank and reduce the daily cash withdrawal limit to a low amount to limit the potential damage you can do if you slip one day. In other words, if you are out and have your card with you to do some shopping and feel the urge to draw money out to go gambling with there is only so much damage you can do.

It can be very frustrating living this way and limiting your exposure to cash but ultimately it is the way to regain control of your finances and regain trust with your loved ones.

Debts.

Being in debt usually comes hand in hand with gambling addiction for most. The amount of money you have wasted so far gambling is unimportant, it is gone and will not be coming back so you need to accept this and move on. Over the 30 years I was gambling, I spent somewhere in the region of three hundred and fifty to three hundred and eighty thousand pounds, or depending on the exchange rate, about half a million dollars. It is not important, it is gone, I will not get it back. Also I would not have made that amount of money if I had lived a normal life because I would not have needed to without a gambling addiction to feed. The only reason I mention the amount is to give people, especially non gamblers trying to understand, an idea of the severity of the addiction and the financial implications. Some people will have spent far more than that and some far less. It is all relative, someone who earns £10,000 a month but spends £20,000 has no bigger a problem than the person earning £1000 but spending £2000.

What is important is to face up to your debts, take responsibility and make a structured plan to pay them off. Being in debt is one of the major triggers for gambling due to the stress it causes and the false belief that it is possible to win enough to pay off any debts. The truth is even if you did win a substantial amount of money that could help pay your debts you would not, you would gamble that away too. Therefore putting together a plan to pay off debts is an important part of your recovery. The good news is that once you stop gambling you will realise that you do have some disposable income, however small, to begin paying debts off and you are no longer accruing more debt.

Each person's scenario and level of debt is going to be different and it would be irresponsible of me to suggest how you should handle it. You should seek professional and free advice from your local government website or Citizens' Advice Bureau if you feel your debt is beyond your control. They will advise about debt management plans, money management, individual voluntary arrangements (IVA), administration orders and bankruptcy. Some solutions will result in poor credit ratings but these can be rebuilt while others could even improve your credit rating which is why it is important to seek the correct advice.

It maybe you do not need advice if you know you can handle your debt yourself, but again, you must be totally transparent about your debts if possible with a loved one and get them involved with your plan to pay them off. There are some practical steps you can take to help such as having an honest conversation with your bank or credit card company if you owe money to them. Explain your situation and ask if they can at least reduce or remove the interest for you to help enable repayment in a timely fashion. If your credit rating has not been destroyed perhaps swap credit card debts to a lower interest card but ensure you close the account of the old one. When any credit card is paid off I recommend closing the account as it reduces temptation and access to funds further down the line. Look to concentrate on getting rid of the highest interest debts you have as quick as possible.

If you have an overdraft, once it is paid off reduce it to a small amount or even zero to limit access. My overdraft was £4500 which is ridiculous when you think about it. Who in the normal, sane world of any family life needs an overdraft of that scale? Overdrafts are supposed to be a financial buffer to help if you slightly mismanage your finances one month to allow everything to go through. I spent years never getting out of my overdraft because my monthly take home pay was nowhere near enough to pay it off and get out of it. The money I lost in interest to the bank each day was crazy. But eventually once I stopped gambling and got my debt plan in place I was able to pay off my overdraft along with all my other gambling debt. And if I could do it then you can do it too.

You will stop gambling and you will pay off your debts and have a normal financial life again. You can even start to put some savings aside for a rainy day or to protect you and your family should any unexpected financial hardships come along. I know that might seem impossible now but trust me, once you stop wasting money gambling you will be surprised at how much you do have. Not having any savings is a common thing for lots of people, not just gamblers, so do not feel bad about having no savings right now if that's the case.

1 in 3 U.K residents do not have more than £600 in savings and nearly 70% of Americans adults have less than $1000 stashed away. Once your most pressing debts are under control I sincerely advise you start to put some savings aside, even £50 a month would put you ahead of the 1 in 3 U.K residents who do not have £600 after a short year. Should some unexpected bill come along that you need money for it will be a huge relief to have it in the bank and mean you will not slip back into old habits of thinking gambling is the way to raise funds. We all know that will only make matters worse.

So remember, get the roadblocks in place between you and access to money and gambling opportunities and get that debt management plan in place. You can do this.

13. THERAPIES FOR GAMBLING

I f you are a problem gambler chances are you will be able to stop gambling on will power alone given the right motivation such as a loved one telling you they will leave you and meaning it. Or the bank informing you they are going to take your house from you if you do not start making mortgage payments. Unfortunately if you are a compulsive gambler, even when faced with dire circumstances such as these, you will not be able to stop using will power alone. Compulsive gamblers will need treatment, therapy, or support if they are to stop and of course a problem gambler will find it easier to stop if accessing the same help which is available also.

There are many different types of therapy or treatments available to help with stopping gambling, some will work for one person but maybe not for another. Some people will have success with just one type of treatment and others with a combination of treatments. Everyone is different and so will be the treatment that suits them best. In any given treatment that you choose, one therapist might suit you better than another even though the basis of the therapy is the same. As I have previously mentioned I have had great success with one hypnotist in the past but just did not gel with another one years later. The same can be said of group support based therapy, the G.A group I attend is fantastic and I have made some incredible friends there, but I have been to other groups and never gone back as it just did not feel quite right for me. So if you do not receive the results you had hoped for with any given therapy try another therapist or group before giving up on it. And if you truly find that a certain type of therapy does not work try another type. Do as many things as you can to rid yourself of the addiction of gambling, give yourself the very best chance available to succeed.

The only result for a compulsive gambler if they do not stop gambling is a life alone and broke, in prison or committing suicide. But it does not have to get to that because there is help and support out there for you to stop gambling and start living again.

In this chapter I will briefly go through the basics of some of the more widely known forms of therapy available to gamblers wishing to stop. If you like the sound of one of them do a little research to see what is available to you and go ahead and give it a try.

Hypnosis.

Hypnosis is useful to help with gambling as it targets emotional and often unconscious triggers that cause you to gamble. It builds your self-confidence and helps to break the patterns of negative thoughts, emotions, and behaviours. This in turn can help to reduce stress and anxiety while also building resilience to deal with things in life that can otherwise cause temptation to gamble.

Hypnosis as a therapy is not what most people think it is, it is not the spectacle you see on television or on stage. You are not going to find yourself dropping your pants every time someone whistles Dam Busters after your first treatment.

When you are under hypnosis you are physically relaxed but mentally aware. Your subconscious mind is very receptive to hypnotic suggestions. You are in complete control the whole time during the session. The hypnotherapist will induce a state of deep relaxation allowing them then to access your subconscious mind and find the roots of your gambling patterns. By then using the power of suggestion they can help you to break these patterns by changing your thought processes and helping you learn to channel your emotions in different, healthier ways.

Counselling.

Counselling is a talking therapy and a learning process in which your counsellor will help you to learn how to deal with your problems and change your way of thinking when it comes to gambling by talking through your thoughts on it. It gives you the opportunity to discuss what's on your mind with a professional, in a safe, confidential, and non-judgemental way. They encourage you to explore your own thinking and reasoning. They help you to focus on the core triggers that cause you to gamble, what it is that compels you to gamble and understand the reasons behind those gambling urges. The more you learn about yourself and your gambling, the more the counsellor can then help you to focus on healthier and more constructive ways to cope with life without resorting to gambling. With the new information that you learn you can begin to understand the things that seem to be out of control in your life and to make good decisions on how best to deal with them.

Cognitive Behavioural Therapy. (C.B.T)

CBT is also a talking based treatment which has been found to be a very effective therapy for gambling. It focuses on cognitive distortions which are habitual negative thought patterns that are both inaccurate and destructive. CBT teaches people to identify, question, and change their negative thoughts and behaviours related to gambling, and respond to problem behaviours generally in a more productive way. This is known as cognitive restructuring and works by highlighting the difference between their distorted beliefs and reality, helping them to understand and accept the difference. In this way the gamblers negative behaviours are changed for positive constructive behaviours.

CBT therapy will also help you to set achievable goals in relation to your recovery. These are small to begin with but will gradually build as you progress in your recovery.

Sessions can be on a one to one basis or in a group, face to face or online, either setting has been found to be equally effective for people. The counsellor will also give you homework to work on through the week between sessions usually in the form of workbooks or some form of journaling. There are many free workbooks to be found online too which can be helpful as an introduction but I would always recommend seeing an actual therapist for the best result.

Support Group Therapy.

Often problem and compulsive gamblers feel as though they are the only ones with this affliction and that they are alone and have no one to turn to who would understand. However you are not alone and support groups are a great way to connect with people going through the same issues as yourself. Speaking to people who are going through similar things as you make a huge difference. Not only does it bring comfort and relief to know you are not the only one but it is a fantastic way to learn what works for others to stop gambling. You can learn through the experience of people within the group and find support and encouragement without any judgement. You can learn to relax and begin to speak freely about gambling and all that means to you. Although there are some heart breaking stories and a lot of pain in those meetings it is also a place full of camaraderie and great humour. It is basically free access to people who have become experts in stopping gambling through life experiences and a hugely important resource to be used to stop gambling.

The most well-known support group is Gamblers Anonymous who have meetings all over the world as well as many online ones. Gamblers Anonymous was started in 1957 in Los Angeles by two men who met by chance and found they shared a troubled history due to gambling. They began to meet on regular basis and found that with the help and support of each other they were able to abstain from gambling were as before they had not. During the course of their discussions they concluded that to prevent relapse they needed to change as people and developed a spiritual set of guidelines to live by to achieve this and maintain their abstinence. They felt it was important to carry this message of hope to other compulsive gamblers and other support groups were formed both in the states and other parts of the world reaching London U.K in July 1964.

Gamblers Anonymous, more commonly known as G.A, is a fellowship of people who support each other through their shared experiences, hopes and strengths. Despite its spiritual guidelines and frequent reference to God and Higher Power these are whatever your understanding of God or Higher power might be.

They are not aligned with any religious or political organisation and welcome all people regardless of age, disability, gender, racial heritage, religious belief, sexual orientation, or identity. The only requirement of joining G.A is a desire to stop gambling and to help others to do the same. What you hear in the room stays in the room and you are expected to show respect to others within the fellowship.

In G.A you are encouraged to attend as many meetings as possible, especially early on in recovery, to utilise the support of the people in the room, to understand you cannot gamble on anything ever again but to take things one day at a time. Like other fellowships G.A offer a 12 step program of recovery with meetings dedicated to this known as Steps meetings. They also run a range of other types of meetings with the most common being known as main meetings where compulsive gamblers sit together and discuss their difficulties and offer one another support.

Residential Support.

Residential Support is very effective for helping to break the pattern of gambling by taking you away from that environment and placing you in a safe and secure residential centre for rehabilitation. As part of an intensive program you will work together with Counsellors and Therapist on a range of techniques and strategies to help you to stop gambling. Residential programs can last up to 3 months though some are shorter at 4 weeks, each is different depending upon the person needing help and their personal circumstances.

Gordon Moody is one centre for structured residential treatment in the U.K but they also offer advice, counselling, and online support to help people recover from gambling addiction. Many other rehabs are available at a range of costs, some more affordable than others but with longer waiting lists. As with anything I would recommend doing your research before committing to anything and speaking with a medical professional to see if they can refer you or at least recommend somewhere.

Medication.

There have been many medical trails around the world to discover if medication can help with Pathological Gambling with the three main areas being serotonin reuptake inhibitors (SRI), opioid antagonists, and mood stabilizers. There have been promising results in all three areas with opioid antagonists seemingly the most effective.

Naltrexone is an opioid antagonist which is widely used to treat drug and alcohol addictions but has been found to be very effective in treating gambling addiction also. Naltrexone helps addicts fight their addictive cravings and has been prescribed in relatively low numbers in the U.K despite its success and only subscribed when other methods fail. It has also been used effectively in other countries around the world but again usually where other types of treatments have failed.

Other medications may be also prescribed such as antidepressants and mood stabilizers to help problems that often go along with compulsive gambling — such as depression, OCD or ADHD. By helping people to overcome these problems they stand a much better chance of then overcoming gambling addictions also.

The National Gambling Treatment Service.

The National Gambling Treatment Service offers help and support to gamblers wishing to stop. It works with, and alongside, the National Health Service. It is free at the point of delivery, provides telephone, online and face-to-face treatment for individuals and groups in Great Britain. Self-referrals can come through the 24/7 National Gambling Helpline (0808 8020 133) for accessing the treatment, which is provided by a network of NHS trusts and voluntary sector organisations.

The National Problem Gambling Clinic in London is part of the National Gambling Treatment Service and is jointly commissioned by GambleAware and NHS England. The system includes other providers such as The Northern Gambling Service with clinics in Manchester and Leeds, GamCare and The Gordon Moody Association.

The NHS Northern Gambling Service works closely with a range of people and organisations including GPs, local councils, NHS trusts, national and local charities, Citizens' Advice, the criminal justice system, debt agencies, substance misuse services and homeless agencies. They can be contacted on 0300 3001490 or found online.

In America the National Problem Gambling Helpline, operated by the National Council on Problem Gambling (NCPG), is available and can be reached via phone or text at 1-800-522-4700. The National Helpline is confidential and available 24 hours a day. Additionally, there is an online helpline chat available on the NCPG website. Each American state has its own hotline available too and should be free to call, details can be found online. I am not aware of what services they offer but I am positive they will signpost to local resources if you need help and are based in the States.

Likewise Australia and other countries around the world with a high rate of problem gambling do have National Gambling hotlines and services to help and a quick internet search should get you in touch with someone who can initiate help for you.

14. WORKING TOWARDS BECOMING THE BEST VERSION OF MYSELF

S o what's changed? Why is this time any different from the other times I tried to stop? Well, I decided that if I was going to stop gambling, I had to change holistically as a person - the person I was before could not stop. I knew I would have to work on my general wellbeing, and also specifically at becoming the best version of myself possible.

I know now that I am a 'better' person than I used to be, but it is an ongoing project and always will be. It has not happened overnight, there is no quick fix, you need to be patient, and realise that although positive change can *begin* to happen at once when you decide that you want it to, there is no instantaneous, complete transformation.

I consider myself to be better than my old self, but certainly no one else. I am no saint and have plenty of flaws, but the crucial difference is that I am aware of them, and work continuously on them, always aiming to change for the better.

I certainly can't tell you how to become the best version of yourself - but I can tell you the things that are working for me, and maybe some will strike a chord with you. I hate to sound like an ageing hippy, but it's so much more about the journey and the things you learn along the way, rather than just the destination.

The first thing I did? Reassess my values. Personal values are the basis for everything; they are at the heart of how you choose to live your life and determine what is most important to you. Values aren't set in stone, and as you move through life you may find your values change depending on circumstances and external factors. Values that you once held as a top priority in life may begin to have less importance. For example, working hard and having a fantastic work ethic might be really important values while pursuing a career. If you then become a parent, the desire for a work-life balance and quality family time might mean the work ethic is no longer top priority.

I concentrated on the values that would make me happy, bring fulfilment to my life, and be a source of pride. Honesty, kindness, forgiveness, generosity, family life, thoughtfulness, love, health, trustworthiness, creativity, compassion, tolerance, acceptance, knowledge, humour, and joy. Most of these values held a place deep down in my heart already but had been overshadowed by the all-consuming value I used to put upon gambling and everything associated with it.

By concentrating on trying to live my life by these positive and healthy values, I knew I could become a better version of myself and improve my general wellbeing. I knew that by doing that, I would feel better about myself, be more confident, be stronger, happier, and therefore give myself the best chance possible to resist gambling.

Whatever you do with regards to living life by your chosen values, it should be activities and goals that are wholesome, actionable, and achievable. If you want to drop bad habits and replace them with good, don't start out with something too big or difficult, or it will become onerous, and something else to worry about. This will most likely result in feeling like you've failed before you've even started. For example, I've found guided meditation and yoga have been fantastic for helping to clear my mind in the past. They have helped with my anxiety, helped me to sleep better and improved my overall wellbeing. But I have never practiced yoga or meditated for hours on end. I started with small, bite-size chunks, little and often, and built from there. I found that even just 10 minutes guided meditation or 15 to 20 minutes yoga on a regular basis was really beneficial. I have never once done meditation or yoga and not felt great after it. Whatever activities or goals you set yourself towards improving your wellbeing, remember to start small and build.

I have spoken to many people who found that when they stopped gambling, they had the time and the desire to do the things they used to love, or to find whole new passions in life. Art, music, reading, writing, knitting, crochet, carpentry, scrap booking, photography, sporting activities, games - there are so many fantastic hobbies and past times out there to discover and try, when you stop gambling you will have the time and energy to try some out.

If you do take up a new hobby or activity as a way of improving your general wellbeing, please don't base your expectations on what you might see on social media or television. Social media only ever shows people at their best, and not their problems and imperfections. Very few people are exceptional at what they do, and that is because it can take a huge amount of work, time, and effort to be exceptional at anything. Very few people have that kind of time to dedicate in their busy lives. Also, you need to love the process of achieving excellence and again very few people do, they only love the idea of the end result. The important thing is how much you enjoy doing something, and the sense of satisfaction you get from improving. Please, only measure improvement against yourself, not others. You do not need to be perfect, few people are, enjoying what you do and just being O.K at something is an individual, personal perfection.

So, what have I done? I've listed below some of the things I've been working on to improve my overall wellbeing. It's by no means definitive, but it might give you some ideas to get you started.

- **Be Honest** - I try to be honest with myself and others. I do believe in the old saying, if you have nothing nice to say about someone say nothing at all.

- **Be Connected** - I try to stay connected with people, even if it is only to pick up the phone now and again to see how they are. Like many of us, between family life and work, there's not much time left for spending with friends, but I try to keep in touch. As my kids get older and have their own lives to lead, I hope to make up for lost time, especially with some of my closest friends from school. Since stopping gambling, I have been fortunate enough to get involved with something called 'Burning Man' in the States. I help to organise a yearly regional event in the UK, which has helped immensely in my recovery, thanks to the wonderful people who I have connected with. My life has been enriched so much through that whole experience and the friends I have made, who are scattered around the globe. It's such a stark contrast to the isolation of gambling. It has really brought out a creative side to me too.

- **Be Generous** - I love the Principle of Gifting, taken from my 'Burning Man' experiences. It's essentially the idea of gifting something - anything from a material item to a simple act of kindness - to another person with no expectation of receiving anything in return, and for no other reason other than it's a nice thing to do to brighten another's day. There's no expectation of reward or recognition for the act, and I have sent gifts all over the world anonymously - although they do sometimes figure out it is from me. I think the reason I like the Principle of Gifting so much is because it is so far removed from the selfishness of gambling. It can cost as much or as little as you can manage, but the impact is huge.

- **Be Helpful** – This one is simple; I try to help other people and to be kind. There is a brilliant book by Dr David Hamilton called "The Five Side Effects of Kindness". Reading this was enlightening, as being kind has been proven to make us happier; it's great for the heart, slows ageing, improves relationships and is contagious. The best thing is it costs nothing. As an old mate of mine always says, "It's nice to be nice".

- **Be positive** - I like to try my best to be optimistic, choose positivity in life and try to look on the bright side. How a person reacts or feels about any given situation is a choice, not always an easy choice, but if you can approach things with positivity it helps immensely.

- **Be Outdoors** - I love to get outside, disconnect from life, and reconnect with nature – usually through going for walks or a cycle ride. I used to absolutely love running, until it caused too many problems with my knee, hip, and feet. Yes, physically, I am falling apart. There was nothing better than putting on my headphones, listening to music and going for a run down the dirt trails and paths along the local canals and river. I found it had a real meditative quality and allowed me to zone out for a while and forget life's problems.

- **Be Open to New Ideas** - I decided knowledge, research, learning and self-development would be key to my recovery. To this end, I have listened to numerous podcasts, audiobooks, and Ted Talks. I've read many books and blogs about gambling, and self-development. All of these helped to fill the void left behind by gambling. There is a wealth of information out there, about everything you might have an interest in. Find what interests you and invest some time in developing your knowledge.

These are just some of the areas in my life that I am working on to improve my general wellbeing and give myself the best chance at staying away from the old mind-set which would inevitably lead back to gambling.

Do not be afraid to give things a go, try anything that takes your fancy, even things you are not sure about, because you will never know how beneficial something might be for you if you do not try it. My own journey of self-development has taken me down some unexpected but wonderful paths.

15. SETBACKS

On the road to recovery its possible you may take a tumble and end up momentarily giving in to the addiction and gambling again. We are compulsive gamblers after all so it is hardly surprising that there may be a slip or a relapse along the way.

We fight daily against it and it is hard and exhausting to do so. All the while the addiction seductively whispering in our ear, like a past lover reminding us of all the good times together. And if we challenge it and remind it of all the bad times, the pain, and the misery we had together, it lies and tells us this time will be different. And so you may in a moment of weakness succumb.

And you may be lost for only a short while or perhaps a number of hours or even days, gambling again. The important thing is once you come out of that gambling session and come to your senses you must immediately dust yourself off after your tumble and get back on that road to recovery. Do not despair and allow the addiction to take over totally once again, it does not mean all your previous hard work counts for nothing, it is merely a setback, do not give in. There may be setbacks along the way, you may lose the odd battle against the gambling addition but overall you can win the war, one day at a time.

So what should you do after a setback or slip? Well I would say the first thing is to reach out to someone and tell them you have slipped. Ideally, if you are part of a support group such as G.A, reach out to another member who will understand and support you. The sooner you reach out the better, call or message and possibly go and meet up with a fellow support group member. Do not be embarrassed to hold your hands up and admit you have had a slip. You are a compulsive gambler after all and any G.A members should realise regardless of their clean time they are only ever one bet away from their own slip. It is the first step after all to admit we are powerless over gambling which in turn is the first step back onto the road to recovery. Take pride in the fact that you have had the courage to reach out and tell others. It is also an example to others on their own path, when they have seen you reach out, hopefully it will give them the strength to reach out for help and support they need themselves if they ever slip.

You could tell a friend or loved one if doing so will not cause them too much pain in turn. Honesty is a huge part of recovery and it is imperative you are honest with your G.A group if you are part of such a group or therapist if you have one. Controversially I am going to say "think carefully" if you need to tell a loved one who might already have a strained relationship with you due to gambling. Assess the damage done and the potential further damage to the relationship if they know. Will they support you and even if they do is it right to hurt or worry them if you have the support of your fellowship? Do not ruin and throw away a relationship with a loved one over one slip. If you have forsaken the path to recovery altogether then tell them, they deserve to know, but that is very different from just one slip.

If you are in treatment with a therapist or counsellor of some type then you should definitely tell them and make an appointment for a session as soon as possible. You may be scheduled in for one in the near future but in this instance you must get in to see them asap as an additional appointment.

Many people starting out on the road to recovery will relapse, its actually part of the journey. I believe each relapse that may occur is an opportunity to learn something. If you analyse the circumstances that brought about your act of gambling this time around there will be something to learn from it. You may think there is nothing to analyse and you just messed up and had a bet. However I guarantee there were things going on that led you to that moment that could have been avoided if you had been vigilant. Vigilance is the answer to complacency.

So what do I mean by complacency? The definition of complacency means a feeling of contentment or self-satisfaction, often combined with a lack of awareness of pending trouble or controversy.

Basically, you thought you were doing really well and you had this gambling thing under control so you inadvertently started doing things or placing yourself in situations that put you in danger of gambling again. Maybe you went back to having access to surplus amounts of cash. Perhaps carrying large amounts of money in your pocket again. When you have the ability to pay for everyday items on smart phones using contact-less you seldom need much more than loose change in your pocket. Or you might have a job that you receive a lot of cash payments and instead of getting them straight into the bank or handed off to a loved one you have been letting it build up at home. Maybe you decided to start carrying your cash card every day and increased the amount you could withdraw daily.

Or you decided it might be handy to get a credit card again now your credit rating has improved just in case you ever need it? Maybe you started associating with old acquaintances or visiting old haunts from your past gambling life because you thought you could now handle to be in that environment.

And perhaps these thoughts were not your own but the addiction setting you up ready for the fall?

Of course there are other factors that can lead you back to gambling such as the everyday struggle of life. Crap job, struggling with finances, relationships going wrong, stress, loneliness, boredom, illness, or bereavement. Rather than have to deal with these things, it is tempting to return to the escapism of gambling. Just because you manage to stop gambling for a period of time does not mean life is still not hard at times. I know this as much as anyone.

In the first six months of stopping gambling my father passed away unexpectedly after a very short but brutal battle with lung cancer. He only knew he had lung cancer for three weeks, the first week of which he never told me because I was going on holiday and he did not want to spoil it for me and my family. That was the kind of great Dad that he was, even in that moment he was thinking of me and not himself. It was the hardest thing I have ever had to deal with, I loved my dad immensely and I will always miss him. Six months after that I had an operation on my hip after a year of suffering with it which meant I was going to be off my feet for six weeks and unable to work for twelve. The day after I got home from the hospital I woke to the find it plastered all over the news that the company I worked for had gone into administration. How the hell was I going to find another job when I could not even walk for six weeks let alone work? So within the first year of stopping gambling I had some major crappy life issues going on that hit me really hard. One thing I knew for certain though was that gambling would only make life worse. I had finally woken up to the fact that trying to escape from my problems by gambling was not the answer. Of course I was also extremely fortunate to have the love and support of my wife to help me through, I know not everyone has something like that in their life.

If you are struggling with life in general then you need to seek advice and talk about it. The G.A. rooms are fantastic for talking through your problems and getting things off your chest. Just having a room full of people who understand you and are supportive listening to your concerns is a huge relief. Someone will usually have a word of advice or a suggestion of what might help as many will have been through similar problems with life as yourself or have ideas about where you might find help. Even if they do not offer advice, often just unloading and getting things off your chest is enough. Do not worry about sharing your problems in G.A. just because they may not be actually gambling related. The idea of any fellowship is to support its members and if you can get support about something problematic in your life which has the potential to lead you back to gambling then you absolutely must talk about it with the group.

If you do not attend G.A. meetings or a similar support group then there are still other people to talk to, friends and family, or if that is not possible there are lots of help lines available. Any internet search engine will get you the information you need to be able to reach out. It does not always have to be a phone conversation if you do not feel comfortable with that, a lot of help lines also have live web-chat or text message services too. There are groups set up on social media and online forums also run by other Gamblers on the road to recovery that you can tap into for support.

Some companies now have confidential employee service help lines which are independent from the company. Your co-workers or line management will not be informed if you call so you can contact them in total confidence. You can discuss with them whatever is worrying you or causing you stress and they can sign post you to the right organisations to help you. These can range from debt management services to counselling, all usually free too. I have personally used this service and found it to be excellent, they arranged a number of telephone sessions of counselling to help me with Anxiety. More and more companies have trained Mental health First Aider's available, I myself have trained to be one in work along with a few other colleagues. A mental health first aider's role in the workplace is to act as a first point of contact for people with mental health issues, providing support and guidance to their colleagues.

So always remember a relapse is an opportunity to learn. Do not beat yourself up about it. Identify the reasons you went back to gambling and put in place whatever roadblocks you need to in order to make sure it does not happen again. If it is practical measures like not carrying cash or avoiding certain people and places then do it. If it is general life getting on top of you then reach out to someone and get some help and relief. Please do not suffer in silence. I cannot stress enough how important it is to talk and get things off your chest.

And remember, no matter how crap life can get, gambling is never the answer and will only make things worse. It is a delusion to think otherwise.

16. LIFE AFTER GAMBLING

So, what does life after gambling look like? It was hard in the past to imagine what life would look like without gambling, never mind after it. But there is such a thing, and it is amazing.

I honestly believe that anyone can achieve a life without gambling and any life without gambling will be better, guaranteed. I want to share with you how my life has changed for the better since I stopped gambling because I want you to know a happy life is possible for you too.

Firstly, I absolutely love the free time I have. I spend time with my loved ones and friends. In fairness, my life is still busy between work and running around with the kids, which is great, but I do not see my friends anywhere as much as I would like to. I do spend much more quality time with my wife and kids, which is fantastic. It's not always about doing something that costs money, like days out to places, but it's about being present when I am with them - not preoccupied with gambling thoughts running around my head. I love going for walks with them and getting some exercise and fresh air, even just up and down the canal or river near to where we live. I love going on long bike rides with my son, my daughter is less keen on this, but I am hoping as she gets older, she will join us more. Playing board games at the dining table for an hour or so, or a game of cards (without the gambling) is great fun.

I am truly happy now, and so thankful for the life I live and the love I have in it. Before, when I was gambling, I did not appreciate what I had. Instead, I thought all the time about gambling, but it was never enough, I could never win enough, I could never satisfy my addiction, and trying to do so was always on my mind. I missed out on so many important things, the things that really matter in life: love, family, friends, health, adventure, travel, creativity, music, and art. These are the things that are in my life now, these are the things that fill the void that gambling left behind, and they bring so much satisfaction and joy.

I no longer worry about debts, bills, credit cards, payday loans, or experience the dread of opening the monthly bank statement. I still have bills and a mortgage to pay, all the usual stuff that a lot of people have, but the point is, I do not worry about them. I can afford them now that I am not gambling and can budget accordingly. I appreciate that I am extremely fortunate to have a good job - without that, I may have some financial worries, but they would still be less than they used to be, now I am not gambling. Not gambling means I have concentrated on my career, been 'present' in my job, and worked much more effectively than I used to. This has led to promotion and a pay rise. I know that many are either unemployed or not paid well, and financial worries are very real - if you are one of these people, I feel for you. I have worked for two large companies that went bankrupt and have spent time out of work with no money to pay the bills. I also know that regardless of anyone's financial worries, gambling can only ever make matters worse.

Since ditching gambling, I have eventually been able to take my family on holidays and travel by myself to the States, all paid for by saving and not putting it on a credit card or getting a loan. In the past, a holiday in Europe or even within my own country, would have been a worry, wondering how I was going to get the money to pay for it, where were the spends going to come from? All that is a thing of the past now that I am not wasting money gambling.

I no longer live-in fear and shame, wondering if and when I'm going to be caught out in a lie. If I say I am going somewhere or doing something, it is the truth because I have no reason to lie. Therefore, I have no reason to be on edge all the time, I do not carry that stress any longer. It is such a weight off my shoulders and so refreshing to live an honest life. It feels so good.

I have found a creative, arty streak, which is something I think maybe I had when I was a child. It was something my dad certainly had; enjoyed painting using water colours and oils. I think he would be proud of me, and appreciate some of my art. My mum thinks so too, which means a lot. I take great joy and pride in creating art, some of which I take to events that I am involved with, to display as part of the décor which people seem to like. I find creating art has a kind of therapeutic quality to it and I can get lost for hours in it.

Now I am not gambling, my mental health is so much better. I still deal with anxiety and lack of self-confidence from time to time, but nowhere near as much as I used to. The mental strain that gambling used to cause was overwhelming at times, and a low-level constant drain otherwise. I still have those cognitive distortions or mind traps trying to trip me up from time to time, but for the most part I see them for what they are and challenge them. I am constantly working on improving my mental health and self-confidence, mainly through self-help books so I can better understand my mind and talking about my problems and worries with others. It is getting better all the time; I am getting better all the time, and this is only possible because gambling is out of my life. Every gambling addict or problem gambler's mental health will suffer while gambling, how could it not? Once you stop, you will have the energy and capacity to begin to improve it. You can become well again, I promise, with the right help and a little patience.

I also have a very strong desire to help others. This is ironic, as for so long, I lacked the ability to help myself. In the past though, I was unable to really help people as much as I wanted to because I was so consumed by gambling. I did help people sometimes, and bizarrely, this was sometimes financially, despite the enormity of my own money problems. I guess it just depended if I was on a winning streak, or if I decided I was in so much debt that a little more wouldn't hurt - maybe it was only to ease my own guilt, who knows?

I have written this book because I really want to help people who are experiencing harm in their lives because of gambling, not just gamblers but anyone affected by gambling harm. I just want to share what I have learnt in my recovery, and to try and briefly explain gambling addiction as I see it, and to show how I was able to stop gambling. In doing so, I can hopefully inspire others to do the same.

It is important to remind anyone reading this book that I am not an academic, a counsellor, a therapist, a lawyer, financial adviser or in any way a professionally qualified person. I am just John, a compulsive gambler and my last bet was January 5th, 2017.

God grant me the serenity to accept the things I cannot change. Courage to change the things I can. And wisdom to know the difference.

Printed in Great Britain
by Amazon